the
baldies'
survival guide

Other books by Tim Collins:

School Rules
Mingin' or Blingin'
Are You a Geek?
The Ginger Survival Guide

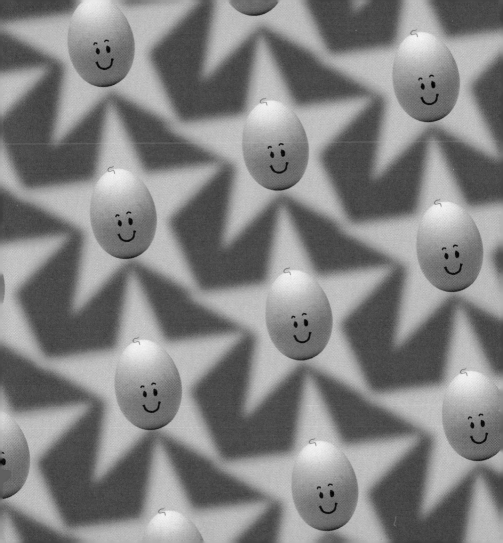

the baldies' survival guide

EVERYTHING THE SLAPHEAD NEEDS TO COPE IN A CRUEL HAIRY WORLD

TIM COLLINS

Michael O'Mara Books Limited

First published in Great Britain in 2007 by
Michael O'Mara Books Limited
9 Lion Yard
Tremadoc Road
London SW4 7NQ

A CIP catalogue record for this book is available from the British Library

Papers used by Michael O'Mara Books Limited are natural, recyclable products
made from wood grown in sustainable forests. The manufacturing processes
conform to the environmental regulations of the country of origin.

ISBN: 978-1-84317-262-8

1 3 5 7 9 10 8 6 4 2

www.mombooks.com

Design, typesetting and illustrations by Envy Design

Printed and bound in Italy by L.E.G.O.

contents

acknowledgements

Thanks to Collette Collins, Chris Maynard, Lindsay Davies and everyone at Michael O'Mara, and to all those chrome domes who shared their inspirational stories about the struggle against baldism.

introduction

There was a time, millennia ago, when man was almost entirely covered in hair. As he slept in caves and ventured out to gather and hunt it protected him from icy winds and violent attacks by hungry beasts. Then, as man evolved and these needs became less pressing, he began to lose this hair. In fact, some men travelled so far along the evolutionary chain that they lost the hair on the top of their heads too. Unfortunately, this clear sign of biological progress angered the less evolved men, and they devised taunts such as 'baldilocks', 'slaphead' and 'chrome dome'. The heads of the bald were compared to boiled eggs and cue balls, and they were sometimes even slapped by Benny Hill fans in cruel acts of copycat violence. The more evolved men were shamed into wearing wigs and hats, and some daring hair engineers even tried to comb their hair from one side of their pate to the other – as though it naturally grew in the shape of Shredded Wheat. Sheep's urine, bat's milk and spider webs were sold as miracle cures for baldness. And some hairless men even went as far as surgery to restore their bonces.

But things have changed now. Perhaps it's down to film stars like Bruce Willis and Vin Diesel. Perhaps it's thanks to sporting icons like Andre Agassi and Michael Jordan. Or perhaps we've all finally admitted that baldness is the true future of human advancement. Whatever the reason, being bald is sexy right now. So sexy, in fact, that many hirsute men deliberately opt for the chrome-dome look.

So the time has come for us to take a moment to reflect (admittedly, most baldies do this all the time) and consider the world of the hairless. Over the following chapters you'll discover everything you need to know about caring for your shiny pate and coping with baldism. You'll also find

the bald facts

Will we ever have a bald Prime Minister again?

Although Blair, Major and Thatcher all visibly receded while in office, the last proper slapheaded PM was Churchill. Since then, both the media and the voting public have shown considerable prejudice against bald politicians. *The Sun* printed a deeply baldophobic front page on the day of the 1992 General Election that featured Neil Kinnock's bald head superimposed onto a light bulb alongside the headline: 'If Kinnock wins today will the last person to leave Britain please turn out the lights?' More recently, the Tories have been criticized for fielding a series of light-on-top leaders who have all failed to cover the centre ground convincingly, including William Hague, Iain Duncan Smith and Michael Howard. Given this recent track record, sadly it's unlikely that either Labour or the Tories will be pitting a baldie against a hirsute candidate in the near future.

out about those shining examples who've truly made a difference to the slaphead community.

So throw away your rugs, hats and miracle cures and display your brilliance to the world – it's time to reclaim your hair-free pride.

the ten best things about being bald

We all know what it's like. You find yourself pulling knotted hair out of the bathroom plughole more often. You realize that bottles of shampoo are mysteriously lasting longer. The top of your head starts to feel colder in the winter and hotter in summer. And each day it takes a little longer to wash your face.

You tell yourself that you've always had a high hairline. You convince yourself that your hair only looks thin because you're combing it in the wrong direction. But the truth is, you're going bald. Your hairline is on a journey to the nape of your neck, and it's not coming back. But rather than get upset about this, why not celebrate the end of the hirsute years? After all, there are plenty of advantages to depilation . . .

You don't have to choose a hairstyle

Although many women find the subject of hairstyling so fascinating they're prepared to read entire magazines devoted to it, most men find choosing a style stressful and pointless. As soon as you've discovered something you feel comfortable with, it goes out of fashion and teenagers openly laugh at you in the street. You only need to look at the example of mullet men for evidence of this. One moment bi-level hair seems like a hip way to hang on to raunchy youthfulness while presenting a respectable front to the world.

The next moment you're so alarmingly outmoded that people are sharing photos of you on the web.

You don't have to go to the hairdressers

Another great thing about avoiding hairstyles is, of course, avoiding hairdressers. For many blokes, a trip to the barber is mildly more enjoyable than a trip to the dentist. You go in asking for a little off the back and sides and emerge with some trendy asymmetrical haircut that makes you look like a bewildered ex-boyband member.

You don't have to worry about going grey

Take solace in the fact that you no longer have to fork out for hair dye, or worry that your barnet is making you look over a certain age. Now that shaved heads are in fashion, with your bare crown you could be almost any age. Handy – you can pretend to be younger when speed dating and older when asking for a promotion.

You'll be perceived as trustworthy

Baldness is also associated with trustworthiness, and quite rightly too. If someone's honest enough to display their receding hairline without recourse to wigs, weaves or comb-overs then they're no doubt upstanding and honest in all other matters too.

You'll be perceived as authoritative

Thanks to wise baldies such as Yoda and Dungeon Master, naked crowns are associated with authority and expertise. We all feel better with a bare-headed head honcho around, and chrome domes often find themselves promoted before their hirsute colleagues. So don't be surprised if you find that your career advances as your hairline retreats.

the bald facts

Do animals go bald?

Although many animals can lose hair due to illness, very few of them undergo a process that can be compared to male pattern balding. Researchers have found that orang-utans, stump-tailed macaques and chimpanzees can experience hair loss when they reach middle age, though it's not yet clear if other members of their species call them 'slapheads'.

In addition to these pilgarlic primates, there are baldie breeds of dog such as the Mexican Hairless and furless cats such as the Sphynx. Although it might be tempting to buy one of these so you can express solidarity with the slapheads of the animal kingdom, you should avoid doing so unless you really want to look like Dr Evil.

You'll be safer at night

Firstly, baldies are perceived to be quite hard, so it's less likely that you'll get mugged or that someone will pick a fight with you. Thanks to decades of skinheads, bouncers, soap characters like the Mitchell Brothers from *EastEnders* and slapheaded supervillains like Lex Luthor, many people now see a bare head as a warning to steer well clear.

And secondly, because *The Highway Code* states that pedestrians should always wear reflective materials at night, the light glinting off your dome will make crossing the road much less hazardous.

You can't get anything nasty in your hair

... such as head lice, the tiny ant-like creatures that feed on your blood and lay up to seven eggs a day in there. Not to mention chewing gum, pigeon shit, baby sick and everything else that causes misery to the hirsute. And, of course, you won't be in danger of setting your hair on fire while downing flaming sambucas like those idiots seen in viral emails.

You'll be joining the baldie mafia

Don't be surprised if your shiny pate puts you at an advantage with fellow members of your oppressed minority group. Slapheaded policemen will let you get away with speeding, baldielocked bank clerks will be uncharacteristically helpful and chrome-domed mechanics and plumbers will spare you the usual scams.

You'll save the world

You won't burn energy with hairdryers, curling tongs and home perming kits and you won't create polluting waste with hair-treatment products. Plus, scientists believe that there may be an even more important way in which baldies can help the planet. At the moment, polar ice sheets that should be reflecting the rays of the sun are melting, and this is worsening the effects of global warming. Perhaps if enough of the human race goes bald we could reflect the rays of the sun and prevent climate change with our very pates.

You don't have to waste time faffing around with your hair

You don't have to comb your hair in the morning, you don't have to check it in the mirror before a date, you don't have to dry it after an unexpected downpour and you don't have to rearrange it after a sudden gust of wind. With all this extra time to get on with their lives, is it any wonder that many baldies achieve so much?

BALD
SPOT

'Hairs are your aerials. They pick up signals from the cosmos and transmit them directly into the brain. This is the reason bald-headed men are uptight.'

Danny, Withnail and I

the causes of baldness

Many theories about the causes of slapheadedness have been put forward over the years. Although the scientific reasons for depilation are generally now accepted, several myths are still bandied about. Here are the bald facts so you can set the record straight.

Baldness is caused by tight hairstyles

It's true that hairstyles that pull back the hair with excessive force can lead to balding. Several hairstyles have been linked to hair loss, including ponytails, cornrows and even the infamous 'Croydon facelift', where women scrape their hair back so tightly that it pulls back the skin on their faces. However, this kind of hair loss is known as 'traction alopecia' and is not the same thing as male pattern baldness. Plus, it's difficult to have much sympathy for the slapheads here. If ponytails, cornrows and Croydon facelifts are the best way you can think of to arrange your hair, it's probably best that it gets confiscated from you.

Baldness is caused by hats

It's possible that traction alopecia could be induced by an especially tight hat if you never took it off, but it's pretty unlikely. Nonetheless, hats were thought to be a major cause of baldness for many years.

Given that male pattern baldness typically leaves hair covering the back and sides of the head, it might have appeared that the snug headgear somehow prevented growth above hat-level, so it's easy to see why this theory once seemed plausible. In fact, an Edwardian doctor even predicted that baldness would become less common if hats went out of fashion. But his prediction wasn't borne out – as hat-wearing declined in the twentieth century, slapheads survived.

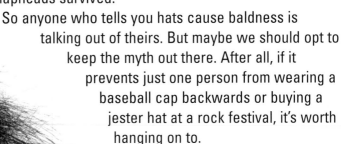

So anyone who tells you hats cause baldness is talking out of theirs. But maybe we should opt to keep the myth out there. After all, if it prevents just one person from wearing a baseball cap backwards or buying a jester hat at a rock festival, it's worth hanging on to.

Baldness is caused by stress

The notion that stress causes baldness can seem like a vicious circle to the hairless. As your forehead expands and your bathroom plughole gets clogged up, you worry about your hair loss and this only serves to make the stuff fall out even quicker. But this is misleading. The type of hair loss that's brought on by stress is called 'telogen effluvium', which is different from male pattern baldness. And it takes a severe trauma to bring it on, so the shock of looking in the bathroom mirror and realizing that you've got slightly more face to wash is unlikely to provoke it.

Baldness is caused by brain activity

The brain being inside the skull has led some to suppose that over-stimulating the grey matter somehow causes hair to fall out. But before you rush off to watch Channel Five or buy a copy of the *Sport* I should point out that there's no evidence of a link between baldness and brain usage. Still, I imagine most slapheads will be quite happy to let this particular myth pass uncorrected.

Baldness is caused by beardiness

It's been suggested that men who grow beards are somehow using up their hair supply and thus are responsible for making themselves bald. There's never been any evidence to suggest a link between the two things in humans, although it has been found to occur in the Play-Doh Barber Shop set.

Baldness is caused by combing or brushing your hair too much

While some balding men would rather look like a receding Robert Smith from The Cure than risk styling their remaining hair, the truth is that both combs and brushes are unlikely to make your hair fall out. So there's nothing to worry about with using either. Unless you're using them to sculpt a comb-over, in which case you should worry, but only from a style perspective.

Baldness is caused by excessive masturbation

The idea that enjoying Mrs Palm and her five lovely daughters too much will make you bald is one of the many myths invented to scare teenage boys. Just to put

Will my hair stay in longer if I stop using shampoo?

It's possible, though unlikely, that hair loss can be caused by an allergic reaction to a constituent of a particular shampoo. Unfortunately, it's not the case that you can halt hair loss by ditching shampoo and leaving your hair to 'wash itself'. You'll still go bald, it's just that you'll look like an especially whiffy road protester while you're doing it.

the record straight, excessive masturbation does not make you go blind, go bald or stunt your growth. However, it can lead to you to developing a suspiciously strong right arm.

Baldness is inherited from your maternal grandfather

Close, but not quite. Baldness does have a genetic heritage, but it can be passed on from either side of your family. The myth that you inherit baldness specifically from your mum's dad has caused many young men to flip nervously through photo albums searching for a nightmare vision of their own chrome-domed future.

Baldness is caused by testosterone

In short, this is true. It's now thought that testosterone reacts with an enzyme present in some men to produce a hormone called dihydrotestosterone (DHT), which causes follicle malfunction. Whether this process occurs in you or not is determined by your genetic makeup, which is inherited from both sides of your family. And ironically enough, the baldness gene is not thought to be a recessive one.

So there we have it. Some men inherit full heads of hair from their fathers and grandfathers, while others inherit bathroom cabinets full of useless cures. So next time a pub loudmouth tries to tell you that baldness is caused by hats, hairstyles or onanism, tell them it's really caused by DHT. Or we could just stick with the myth that it's caused by using your brain too much. Well, I won't tell anyone if you don't.

BALD SPOT

'Dear God, give a bald guy a break. Amen.'

Homer Simpson,
The Simpsons

the baldie hall of fame:
great baldies in history

Many members of the bald fraternity take pride in knowing how many great men throughout the ages have been follicle-deficient. But how much do you know about your hairless heritage?

Don't worry if you need to brush up on your brush-dodgers. The baldie hall of fame is here to celebrate the lives of those slapheads who have shone brilliantly even when they weren't standing next to a lamp.

First up, here's an overview of some dihydrotestosterone-filled greats who've made their mark on history.

William Shakespeare

Most portraits show that the Bard had an exposed crown, although Joseph Fiennes shamefully portrayed him with a full head of hair for *Shakespeare in Love*. Still, the subject of baldness seems to have been important to Shakespeare, and is mentioned in many of his plays. In Act II Scene ii of *The Comedy of Errors* he even points out that baldies save money on haircare. And that was before they'd invented super rich protein-replenishing moisturizing conditioner.

Samson

Old Testament hardman who could wrestle lions, tear down buildings and kill entire armies of Philistines with just the jawbone of a donkey when he had hair, but became weaker than a Hale and Pace punchline without it. The legend of Samson is the most likely inspiration for the myth that long hair is a symbol of virility, which is still tragically adhered to by pro-wrestlers and heavy-metal guitarists.

Aeschylus

According to legend, Greek playwright Aeschylus died when an eagle mistook his bald crown for a rock and dropped a tortoise on it. However, before you all demand a special tortoise clause in your life-insurance policies, let's remember that this story is very unlikely to be true. For a

the bald facts

What is hair?

Hair is an outgrowth of dead cells found on the skin of mammals. Each shaft of hair is made up of a protein called keratin, and grows from holes underneath the scalp called follicles that are supplied with water, minerals and vitamins by capillaries.

So basically hair is just a load of dead stuff hanging off your head, and it's not really worth making a fuss about. Much better to display a polished, pristine pate to the world than leave a load of expired cells dangling from it.

start, Terry Nutkins never encountered any problems like this when filming *The Really Wild Show*. Plus, there seems to be a tradition of attributing ridiculous and unverifiable deaths to the Greeks, as with the philosopher Chrysippus, who supposedly laughed himself to death after getting a donkey pissed and then watching it trying to eat figs. Which, admittedly, does sound quite funny.

Charles the Bald

Ninth-century king of France who deserves his place in this hall of fame on account of his brilliant name. Unfortunately, scholars now think it likely that Charles the Bald actually had a full head of hair, and that his epithet was a joke. In other words, it was the medieval precursor to Eric Morecambe pretending Ernie Wise's hair was a wig by pointing at it and saying 'You can't see the join.'

Interestingly, the monarch's name lives on today as a gay slang term for the male member. Poor bloke. He spends his life in charge of a whole country and gets remembered only as a euphemism for a body part he didn't even resemble.

Various philosophical baldies

The bare-crowned look has never been out of fashion with philosophers, whose pates seem to support the Victorian notion that if you think about things too much your brain will expand and force all the hair off your head.

A tradition of hairlessness can be traced throughout Western philosophy, from Ancient Greeks like Plato, Aristotle and Socrates to post-hirsute postmodernists Jean Baudrillard and Michel Foucault. They spent their lives questioning what really existed. What can't be questioned is that their hair did not.

Hippocrates

The Ancient Greek physician, often referred to as 'the father of medicine', was a celebrated chrome bonce. So celebrated in fact, that the horseshoe-shaped fringe of hair often found on baldies is known as 'the Hippocratic Wreath'. The subject clearly being close to his heart, Hippocrates tried to concoct a baldness remedy consisting of pigeon droppings, horseradish, beetroot and nettles, which sounds more likely to cover your head in an unpleasant rash than hair. However, he got closer to the mark in *The Aphorisms of Hippocrates*, in which he observed that eunuchs don't go bald, now known to be due to their lack of testosterone. Thankfully, though, he stopped short of recommending castration as a baldness prevention.

Elisha

An extreme example of fighting baldism is related in the second Book of Kings in the Old Testament, where the prophet Elisha is teased by a group of children:

'And as he [Elisha] was going up by the way, there came forth little children out of the city, and mocked him, and said unto him, go up, thou bald head; go up, thou bald head. And he turned back, and looked on them, and cursed them in the name of the LORD. And there came forth two she-bears out of the wood, and tore forty and two children of them.'

So, apparently, God thinks that baldism is so sinful that He's prepared to send bears out to kill anyone who's guilty of it. While even the most dedicated bald-rights crusader might consider this an overreaction, you only need to look at the deity's own thinning white hairdo to understand why He's so sensitive about the issue.

Caligula

According to the historian Suetonius, baldie Roman emperor Caligula was so jealous of the hirsute that he would order them to shave their heads. It seems unlikely that any chrome-domed leader could get away with behaviour like this today, although maybe Kinnock, Hague or Duncan Smith were planning to do it when they reached office. We'll never know.

Winston Churchill

Perhaps the greatest-ever British baldie, Churchill resisted both the encroachment of the Nazis on Britain and the encroachment of artificial hairpieces on his bonce. And what war-torn nation wouldn't have felt more reassured by his proud gleaming dome than the ridiculous side-parted hair of his arch-nemesis, Hitler?

The Millennium Dome

It's no surprise that after all this baldie achievement, the Government decided to mark the start of the third millennium by constructing a huge hairless dome. Unfortunately, rather than filling it with exhibitions celebrating the achievements of comb-dodgers, they had a few trapeze artists and some displays about transport and the human body, so nobody went.

BALD SPOT

'God made a few perfect heads. The rest have hair.'
US bumper sticker

the patterns of male baldness

The progressive thinning of hair that typically occurs in middle age, which, as we've seen, is caused by hormonal and genetic factors, is known as 'androgenetic alopecia', to distinguish it from other types of hair loss caused by illness or stress.

For some men the process starts with a receding hairline (or, as optimists call it, an 'advancing headline') that is most pronounced at the temples. This creates the V-shaped hairline known as the 'widow's peak', which will make you look like a vampire if you've got especially pale skin. As the temples recede further, the V-shaped strip can turn into a thin strip of hair that resembles an elegantly trimmed lady garden.

For other men, the hairline recedes most quickly in the centre to create the 'naked crown' style, which is a kind of inverse Mohican, with a bald strip in the middle of the head circled by hair on both sides. Men who find their hair decreasing in this pattern are often tempted to experiment with comb-overs, as there is only a thin bald strip to cover. But be warned that such manoeuvres can prove addictive, and you could soon find yourself combing all the way across from one ear to the other in the classic Bobby Charlton style.

Alternatively, the whole of your hairline can recede evenly, and form the style known as the 'domed forehead'. This can be especially unfortunate

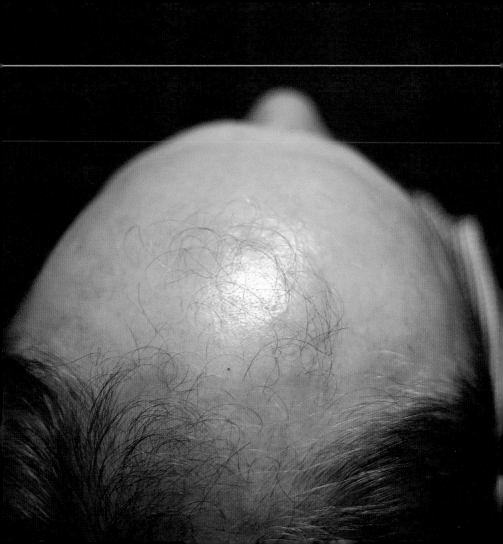

for men whose foreheads jut out, as they end up looking like the Ferengi from Star Trek.

For other men, hair loss can begin with a bald patch on the top of head, of which they are sometimes blissfully unaware. John Cleese claims that he found out he was losing his hair when he spotted a man with a 'terrible bald patch' in a training film he was making, only to realize that the man was himself. So if a friend has bought you this book as a present, and you can't work out why they thought it would be your kind of thing, it's probably a good idea to take a look in the mirror when you get home.

Of course, these patterns of hair loss can occur simultaneously, as with those blokes who have both a bald patch and thinning temples, and who end up with a large McDonalds logo on the top of their bonces. As follicle failure presses on, this can then develop into a wispy frontal patch of hair surrounded by bare skin that resembles a lonely tumbleweed blowing through a desert after a particularly bad joke.

If you're the owner of one of these frontal hair tufts, it's probably not a good idea to grow it long and arrange it in front of the mirror. You might think you've created the illusion of a full head of hair. Others will simply see a bizarre hair sculpture surrounded by a vast expanse of bare skin.

Whatever pattern your hair disappears in, however, the chances are that it will eventually leave you with the short fringe of hair at the back and sides known as 'the horseshoe'. When you find yourself left with just this minimal hairstyle, for God's sake don't grow it so long that you look like Dungeon Master from *Dungeons and Dragons*. Just face the fact that the game is up. Cancel your next appointment with the barber and admit that you and he will have no further dealings. Instead, spend your money on some razors or an electric shaver, and follow the head-shaving guide on page 136. In just a few minutes, you'll be able to shred your remaining strands and face the world as a sexy smoothie.

BALD SPOT

'I'm a man and I will beat up anybody who tries to tell me that I am not a man just because my hair is thinning.'

Bruce Willis, actor

baldie insults

A hair-raising number of abusive terms have been devised over the years to describe the bald. *The Baldies' Survival Guide* believes you should be made aware of any offensive terms you could encounter so that you will be mentally prepared to make a witty comeback, but sensitive readers are warned that they may find the reproduction of these slurs upsetting.

**RATINGS KEY:**
  1 = Inoffensive | **2** = Mildly upsetting | **3** = Unacceptable | **4** = Offensive | **5** = Hate crime

'Bald eagle'

It's no surprise that a creature with the word 'bald' in its name provides ammunition for unimaginative taunters. What is surprising, however, is that bald eagles themselves aren't really bald – their heads are actually covered in white feathers. You could try pointing this out if someone calls you a 'bald eagle', but you could well be digging yourself in deeper.
Baldism rating:

'Baldilocks'

It's not clear why this fairytale-punning insult has become so popular, though the mental image of the comb-avoider in question skipping through some woods to go and steal porridge off some bears probably has something to do with it.

Baldism rating:

'Boiled egg'

An offensive slur, comparing a smooth cranium with the classic breakfast foodstuff. In cases of extreme baldophobia, it can be accompanied by assailants tapping nearby bald heads with spoons as if they were actual boiled eggs. Clearly, the bald community must do all it can to prevent these kind of attacks. That's why *The Baldies' Survival Guide* is conducting the first ever spoon amnesty, as detailed at the back of the book. Please make sure you and all your baldophobic acquaintances take part, so we can eradicate cutlery crimes for good.

Baldism rating:

'Bonehead'

An unpleasant slur that, in contrast to 'egghead', implies both baldness and stupidity. Fortunately, it's one of the easiest bald slurs to respond to, with a simple 'At least I'm not a dickhead / knobhead / pisshead', etc. Touché.
Baldism rating:

'Coot'

An insult that derives from the simile 'as bald as a coot'. As with 'bald eagle', the term is pretty inaccurate, as coots actually have a patch of white feathers on their heads. You could point this out to your abuser, and suggest a more apt comparison, such as 'cue ball' or 'billiard ball', but you'd probably live to regret it.
Baldism rating:

'Egghead'

Not such a bad term in itself, as it can refer to both baldies and intellectuals. This can develop, however, into the more offensive 'boiled egg', as detailed above.
Baldism rating:

'Chrome dome'

A rhyming variation on 'shiny head'. This insult is based on the popular notion that all bald heads are incredibly shiny, and the more advanced insulter may accompany this with the action of pretending to use your head as though it were a mirror. No particular retort is needed if someone does this to you. After all, you'll be perfectly placed for a textbook headbutt.

Baldism rating:

'Dungeon Master'

An insult that was levelled at short baldies following the broadcast in the eighties of the cartoon *Dungeons and Dragons*, especially if the victim was prone to uttering wise but cryptic remarks. Mercifully, the nickname has mostly fallen from use now, although sadly the similar 'Yoda' remains popular.

Baldism rating:

BALD SPOT

'Given the choice between two bald presidential candidates, the American people will vote for the less bald of the two.'

G. Vance Smith

'Pilgarlic'

Although not widely known now, this baldie synonym was popular in the seventeenth century, and is a compound of 'pil' (the spelling of which later changed to 'peel'), and 'garlic'. In other words, the term compared bald heads to peeled heads of garlic, in the days before more accurate comparisons (such as to ping-pong balls) were available.

Baldism rating:

'Ping-pong ball' / 'Cue ball' / 'Billiard ball'

A series of insults that compare bald heads to spherical objects. The first even comes complete with its own chant, which involves repeating '[name of baldie] has a head like a ping-pong ball' to the tune of the William Tell overture. It's not quite clear why this particular operatic piece was chosen to taunt the hairless, but as chants go, at least it's more imaginative than 'Baldie baldie baldie! Oi! Oi! Oi!'

Baldism rating:

'Skinhead'

The term 'skinhead', which is commonly used to describe right-wing nutters from the seventies, can also refer to baldies, as in the old playground chant:

'Skinhead skinhead over there
What's it like to have no hair?
Is it hot or is it cold?
What's it like to be so bald?'

This association between the depilated and the far right seems especially unfair given the number of prominent leftie slapheads there have been, from Lenin to cat-impersonating Respect MP George Galloway. If anyone uses this term to describe you, point out that you have no hatred of minority groups, but they, on the other hand, are oppressing you for belonging to the minority group of baldies. That should shut them right up.
Baldism rating: ⬤⬤⬤⬤⬤

'Slaphead'

The most popular and enduring baldie slur, 'slaphead' is often accompanied by the gesture of the insulter pulling back their own hair and slapping their forehead. However, this can all too easily descend into attacks on your own dome. If this happens to you, let onlookers know that a Benny-Hill-inspired hate crime is being perpetrated and that it should not be tolerated in this day and age.

Baldism rating: ⬤⬤⬤⬤⬤

'Spooner' / 'spoony'

An insult based on the notion that baldies have heads as round and shiny as spoons. This jibe doesn't seem to be related to the spoon attacks described in the 'boiled egg' entry above, but I'm sure it's only a matter of time before some evil genius combines the two.

Baldism rating: ⬤⬤⬤⬤

coping with baldism

Over the past few decades, society has made great advances in combating many forms of terrible prejudices. Yet abuse and discrimination towards the bald remains largely unchallenged.

In fact, baldness seems to be the one physical attribute that everyone still feels comfortable quipping about. Those who would never dream of joking about skin colour, disability or weight think nothing of hurling around terms such as 'cue ball' and 'slaphead'. And it doesn't stop at verbal attacks. Happy slappers have been known to target the hairless with the intention of recording a 'baldie slap' on their mobiles. And there have even been incidents of attackers drawing smiley faces on the back of bald men's heads when they've fallen asleep on the bus.

But how should you respond if you're the victim of baldist abuse?

You can laugh it off

Some chrome bonces will attempt to turn the insult around with well-worn retorts like 'I'm not bald, this is a solar panel for a sex machine' or 'Grass doesn't grow on a busy street.' But by entering into this kind of banter, you're only opening yourself up to comebacks like 'Grass doesn't grow on concrete either.' At any rate, laughing along with baldists only serves to legitimize their hate crimes.

You can be silent

Many shiny-crowned men will simply pretend not to hear the insults aimed at them, but their silence only encourages baldophobia and makes this small-minded prejudice seem acceptable.

the bald facts

Are baldies more intelligent?

Yes. Well, that's what we used to believe, anyway. Victorians thought that overusing the brain caused it to expand, and that this in turn caused hair to fall out. Their 'evidence' for this included the observation that the vast majority of women, who use their brains less, don't go bald. No wonder the emancipation of women was so strongly resisted – the Victorians must have been plagued with nightmare visions of their wives returning home from the office with comb-overs.

It's certainly easy to think of men who were eggheads in both senses, from Plato and Aristotle to Heinz Wolff from *The Great Egg Race*. But sadly, we now know that hair loss is caused by dihydrotestosterone and not by shoving too many facts into your noodle. If there's a correlation between bright minds and shiny heads, it's probably just that clever people realize that bald is beautiful and make no effort to cover their pates.

You can violently attack your abuser with extreme prejudice

Violence might seem like the answer when you're facing follicle prejudice, but it will only serve to reinforce negative bald stereotypes. Remember, it's baldies who are more highly evolved. Rather than stooping to the Neanderthal level of the hirsute, let's practise the non-violent resistance of baldie icon Mahatma Ghandi.

You can think of a comeback

Depending on the situation (i.e. not when you're alone at night and have been accosted by a gang of hoodies), it may be best to respond to baldist attacks verbally. This can entail anything from the Wildean 'Better to have nothing on the top of the head than nothing inside it' to the Liam Gallagherean 'Piss off'. Some baldies have even been known to inflict guilt upon their oppressors by implying that their hair loss is a result of medical treatment rather than pattern balding, but this seems a tad unnecessary.

Perhaps the most effective response to your attacker is simply to comment on his hairstyle. After all, he brought up the topic of hair, and it should be possible to mock his style in some way. Does he have a mullet? Does he have a 'bowl cut'? Is he a ginger? Does his hair make him look like a lesbian? Whatever the style, you can always turn to them and say, 'Well, if I did have hair, I wouldn't do *that* with it.'

If no hair comebacks spring to mind, you could switch your attention to the facial features of your attacker and say, 'If I wanted to do something about my baldness I could buy a toupee. But there's nothing you can do about your face.'

You can report the incident to the police

If you're the victim of physical violence, you can report the incident to the police. Sadly, though, if your attack is purely verbal, it's unlikely that you'll be able to press charges, and you could even get arrested yourself for wasting police time. None of this should be surprising, however, in a legal system so riddled with baldophobia that judges are actually forced to wear wigs.

BALD SPOT

'"Bald asshole"? That's a hate crime.'

Larry David,
Curb Your Enthusiasm

the baldie hall of fame:
tv baldies

In the early days of television there were plenty of unfurnished pates on display. Most BBC programmes were presented by receding, moustached authority figures yapping the Queen's English into oversized microphones. Sadly, the hirsute took over as the medium became more youth-focused. But there are a select few baldies who have braved the glare of the studio lights and who project a positive image of hairlessness.

Telly Savalas

Savalas's bulbous dome was so striking that the name of his character, 'Kojak', remains a byword for 'baldie' to this day. Savalas was bald by choice rather than through follicle malfunction, opting to stick with the cue-ball look he adopted as Pontius Pilate in *The Greatest Story Ever Told* (1965). But wannabe pilgarlic though he was, Telly remains one of the most iconic baldies ever to grace the er . . . telly. Savalas died

in 1994, although not, as a joke at the time had it, because King Kong had used him as a roll-on deodorant.

Brian Moore

Although thinning sports commentators have been anything but thin on the ground, the late Brian Moore is the only one whose baldness was immortalized in song, with the line 'Brian Moore's head looks uncannily like London Planetarium' in the 1986 Half Man Half Biscuit song 'Dickie Davies Eyes.' Fittingly, he retired after commentating on one of the great bald sporting moments – the 1998 World Cup final when Zidane scored twice with his moulting crown.

the bald facts

When do most blokes go bald?

According to a study, male pattern baldness can be observed in about 5 per cent of men by the age of 20, 20 per cent by the age of 30, 50 per cent by the age of 50 and 80 per cent by the age of 70, although these percentages are much lower in some ethnic groups. So, while it might seem like bad luck to go bald young, look on the bright side. You'll be getting the seemingly inevitable hair-loss process out of the way sooner rather than later, and you'll be able to cover your pate with trendy headgear like baseball caps, bandanas, do-rags or hoodies without looking like an uncle dancing at a wedding.

Homer Simpson

It's a source of much pride to the bald community that the greatest TV character ever created is a chrome dome. Many episodes have centred around Homer's hairlessness, but the most famous is probably 'Simpson and Delilah'. In it, Homer buys a re-growth drug called Dimoxinil (an anagram of the genuine drug Minoxidil) and claims it back on company insurance on the grounds that it prevents his brain freezing. This has since

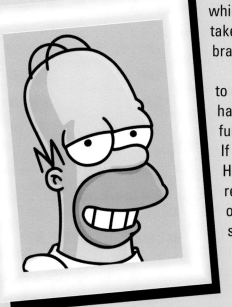

caught on as a bit of baldie-baiting, which goes along the lines of 'Don't take any notice of him, it's just his brain freezing.'

As well as allowing the show to deal with baldie issues, Homer's hair loss also serves a more basic function for creator Matt Groening. If you look closely at a side view of Homer, you'll see that the remaining zigzag of hair on the side of his head and the ear below it spell out the initials 'MG'.

Clive James

Expatriate, ex-hirsute presenter of *Clive James on Television*. According to Janet Street-Porter, James's obsession with the way he looked on screen once drove a cameraman to shout, 'Look Clive, what do you want me to eliminate, the double chin or the bald head? I can't do both.' But given that James has always been a passionate advocate of slapheadedness, and even wrote an article for *The Observer* in 1977 entitled 'Baldies of the World Come Out', we should ignore Street-Porter's jibes and allow him into this hall of fame.

Larry David

Comedian Larry David displays great dedication to the baldie cause on his show *Curb Your Enthusiasm*, in which he makes extensive speeches about the plight of the hairless. In the episode 'The Grand Opening', he even sacks his bald chef for the traitorous act of wearing a toupee. In fact, David only misses out on true slaphead icon status for leaving his remaining horseshoe of hair to grow long and fluffy so that he resembles a fairground gonk.

Arthur Lowe

Glabrous actor who played Captain George Mainwaring in the sitcom *Dad's Army* between 1968 and 1977. Although the show remains hugely popular, some have accused it of baldism, especially the episode 'Keep Young and Beautiful', in which Mainwaring sports a wig to look younger. But let's not forget that Lowe also provided all the voices for the children's show *Mr Men*, which portrayed bald characters such as Mr Happy in a much more positive light than hirsute characters such as Mr Fussy and Mr Clumsy.

Patrick Stewart

Unlike his rug-clad predecessor William Shatner, Patrick Stewart wasn't afraid to baldly go where no man had gone before. While out there, he met many slapheaded aliens, such as the Ferengi, who had knobbly bald heads due to their four-lobed brains, and the Klingons, who cultivated the kind of receding mullets seen mainly in Mid-West shopping malls, country-music concerts and monster-truck festivals in our own universe.

John Cleese

The lanky comic has said that although he's had a huge bald patch since his early thirties, few people notice it due to his height. While it's true that many tall baldies are spared taunts such as 'cue ball' and 'chrome dome', they do have to put up with questions like 'What's the weather like up there?' and 'Did your parents put you in a grow bag?' So it's not that much better, really.

Phil Silvers

As fast-talking, comb-dodging Sergeant Bilko, Phil Silvers outwitted his hirsute rivals to become one of the all-time great TV slapheads. All of which made it especially upsetting for the bald community when the show's cartoon equivalent *Top Cat* used a hirsute yellow feline for the lead role. Many felt that Bilko's baldness was such an important part of his character that a hairless breed of cat such as a Sphynx should have been used.

Jackie Wright

Jackie Wright was the recipient of more than two decades of abuse as the sidekick on *The Benny Hill Show*. Hill's mistreatment of Wright lead to a spate of copycat attacks involving baldies being slapped on the head and then kicked up the arse. Mercifully for the hairless community, the show was cancelled in 1989, although apparently that had more to do with complaints about sexism than baldism.

BALD SPOT

'The good Lord only gave men so many hormones, and if others want to waste theirs growing hair that's up to them.'

John Glenn,
astronaut

miracle cures

The search for a baldness cure has been going on ever since Neanderthal man first noticed that the hair above his eyes wasn't as thick and lustrous as it used to be. Since then, all manner of tat has been peddled by shysters preying on the vanity and insecurity of the bald, and thousands of myths about hair restoration have been circulated.

Shaving your hair

The idea that shaving hair makes it grow back thicker remains surprisingly popular. It's simply not true that feigning a lack of interest in your hair will somehow make it want to return. This is an outgrowth of dead cells we're talking about here, not an ex-girlfriend.

Hypnosis

Many hypnotherapists offer courses and CDs that aim to put you in a trance-like state in order to prevent your hair from falling out. But if this really works, how come Paul McKenna is as bald as a coot? If the best hypnotist around can't save his own hair, what chance has a poxy CD got of convincing your follicles to keep up the fight?

Vacuum caps

In the early twentieth century, a number of companies marketed caps that sucked the blood to the top of the head in order to encourage the hair to grow back. But before you go reaching for the hoover attachment to try to replicate this method, I should point out that these devices achieved little more than making their wearers look like they were about to be executed for first-degree gullibility.

Standing on your head

It was once believed that standing on your head would increase the flow of blood to your follicles and thereby cause hair to re-emerge. Sadly, this theory has now been discredited, but you'd still be better off doing this than replying to one of those spam emails promoting a new 'hair-loss medical breakthrough'.

Bears' grease

The fat of bears was long thought to have been a particularly effective cure for baldness, and references to its effectiveness have been found in medical books from the twelfth through to the eighteenth centuries. Perhaps the logic was that bears are hairy, so rubbing their fat on your head would make you hairy too. Although by that token, wouldn't grease from highland cattle, longhaired cats and the armpits of German women be more effective?

Being hit on the head

In May 2007, a study conducted at the University of Pennsylvania showed that mice had the capacity to regenerate follicles when their skin was wounded. This led them to suggest that a similar process could occur in humans. Sadly, *The Sun* chose to report the story as, 'Scientists have found a new cure for baldness – being hit on the head.' For God's sake, let's try and knock this one on the, er, head before it catches on. The last thing we need is to give the world an excuse for baldie slapping.

the bald facts

Why do monks shave their heads?

Tonsure, the practice of shaving the head in preparation for becoming a monk, is found in both Christianity and Buddhism. It was initially meant to be a renunciation of worldly fashion, but perhaps they should review this now that baldness is trendy. Certainly, the 'Roman Tonsure' style of shaving just the top of the head is still unique to monks, but the 'Oriental Tonsure' style of shaving the entire head looks too hip now. If monks really want to show that they're renouncing worldly fashion, why don't they all get feather-cut mullets with blonde highlights?

Magic

An incantation for curing baldness was engraved by the Assyrians on a clay tablet in the Great Library of Nineveh in the seventh century BC. You're welcome to seek it out and give it a go, of course. But if neither good magician Paul Daniels or evil magician Aleister Crowley could prevent their heads from going bald, I doubt the rest of us have much hope.

Sheep shit

Proving that quack baldness cures have always been around, Roman author Pliny the Elder describes such a remedy in his book *Natural History*, the ingredients of which consisted of sheep dung, frog ashes and honey, which these days sounds more like a variety of Body Shop shampoo than an amazing cure.

It seems that men have tried rubbing most things into their head at one point or another, considering that bat's milk, python fat, mole blood, donkey teeth, sheep's afterbirth, stale urine, spider webs and crushed housefly have all been touted as baldness cures. If you're a great believer in herbal remedies, you might want to get hold of some of this stuff and stick it on your own head. It might not cure your baldness, but at least no one will come near enough to you to find out whether you're bald or not.

Comb-overs

The practice of combing your hair across your bald patch to create the illusion that you have a luxuriant head of hair, whereas you've just decided to comb it in an extraordinary way. Comb-overs are a totally effective baldness cure, with their only slight disadvantage being that they look completely ridiculous when it's windy. And when it's not windy. See 'The Comb-over Question' on page 69 for more on this bizarre ritual.

Wigs

A cowardly method of covering your baldness that, in most cases, is about as convincing and effective as spraying the top of your head with Silly String. See 'The Rug Problem' on page 60 for more on the shameful practice of syrup-sporting.

Dead mice

An ancient Celtic remedy that involved filling an earthenware vessel with dead mice, burying it for a year and then rubbing the contents on a hairless head.

Unsurprisingly, rotten dead mice have now fallen out of favour as a baldness cure, although some wig-wearers keep the tradition alive by *appearing* to sport some kind of deceased rodent on their heads.

Weaves

A weave is a hairpiece that is sewn into your remaining hair to cover up bald areas. Although weaves can look quite convincing at first, they're pretty high maintenance. As your genuine hair grows, it pushes the hairpiece upwards and creates an odd bi-level hairstyle than even the most adventurous New Romantic would have baulked at.

Surgery

Although it's hard to deny that chopping off a bit of your scalp that still sprouts hair and re-planting it on a bald area can be effective, you'd have to have a rather severe hatred of your hairlessness to bother. You'll spend thousands of pounds, put yourself through immense physical pain, and all for an effect that can look pretty unnatural. Surely learning to live with the odd jibe is less hassle than turning yourself into a living patchwork quilt?

Drugs

Like baldie icon Pac Man, many hairless men run around trying desperately to save themselves by munching every pill in sight. Although thousands of drugs have been marketed as baldness cures, only two have ever been approved by the US Food and Drug Administration. The first, Minoxidil, marketed as 'Regaine' or 'Rogaine', comes as a lotion that's applied to the scalp. The second, Finasteride, which is marketed as 'Proscar', comes in pill form. Although both drugs have been found to encourage some re-growth, they won't work for everyone. And even if they do work for you, the results will only last as long as you take the drug, so your wallet will get thin even if your hair doesn't.

Needless to say, true baldie crusaders shouldn't be concerning themselves with any of these cures in the first place. After all, hair is nothing more than a load of dead cells hanging off the top of your crown. It's much better to save yourself money and hassle and display your smooth, gleaming pate to the world.

BALD SPOT

'What he [Father Time] have scanted men in hair he hath given them in wit.'

Shakespeare,
The Comedy of Errors

the rug problem

Nothing offends the slaphead community more than men who cover their beautiful gleaming bonces with wigs. As well as signifying dishonesty, toupees rarely make their wearers look as thrusting and dynamic as they suppose. Would you really look better with a dead animal strapped to your head than a natural shiny dome?

Of course not. But wigs have been an inevitable part of the bald experience for centuries. The Greeks had them, the Romans had them, and the Ancient Egyptians even wore black woollen ones that were short on the top and long at the back, anticipating the invention of the mullet by 4,000 years.

The real heyday of the hairpiece was in the seventeenth century, when large periwigs were in vogue for both men and women. However, this fashion is likely to have been caused by the desire to avoid head lice and conceal hair loss resulting from syphilis rather than embarrassment about pattern baldness. But whatever the reason, this was truly the era of the wiggie, with huge constructions of human or horse hair pretty much a sartorial requirement for anyone of high social standing. Wigs declined in popularity after the eighteenth century, and shamed baldies resorted to hats to cover their naked domes.

It wasn't until the mid-twentieth century that wigs became popular again, and the rug as we know it today was established. However, unlike

the seventeenth century periwig, these toupees are simple synthetic hairpieces intended to deceive onlookers into believing the wearer is hirsute. Quite aside from the accusations of vanity and insecurity that will be cast your way if your deception is uncovered, wigs entail a number of practical problems.

Most famously, of course, is the problem of fixing your wig to your head. Even with the strongest glues and tapes, wiggies have much cause to be nervous on windy days, and enjoying rollercoasters and bungee jumps is right out of the question. With the extreme weather that global warming is bringing about, wigs are looking like a more dangerous option all the time.

Then there's the question of finding a wig that blends in with your natural hair. Few *rugmeisters* ever manage achieve the magic combination of colour match, texture match and lack of join visibility, and just one day of careless application can lead to a lifetime of taunts like 'shag-pile head' and 'astroturf'. Especially if you're a teacher.

There are also a few subtler considerations for the would-be wiggy. How do you suddenly go from a receding hairline to a full head of hair? Do you introduce your wig via a series of smaller ones, as if your hair was magically growing back?

Also, how do you account for the fact that your hair stays exactly the same length all the time? Some more committed hair-fraudsters have been known to rotate a series of wigs of different lengths, to maintain the illusion that they are growing and cutting their hair at regular intervals. But is it really worth going to all this effort just to maintain the illusion of functioning follicles? How do you account for never losing your hair as you age? Surely you should cut your wig to recede a tiny bit each year if you're to maintain your pretence?

In short, wigs aren't worth the hassle, and are only worn by those who are too cowardly to flash their naked pates to the world. But if you must wear one, at least do it properly and get a seventeenth-century-style periwig. The sight of you strolling regally down the street with a huge horse-hair construction covering your entire upper body will be enough to shock any potential rugspotters into silence.

SUPER GLUE

NET WT. 0.11 OZ. (3g)

the baldie hall of shame:
rug addicts

To the bald and proud, wearing a wig would seem to involve an incredible amount of effort for results that are at best questionable. But here are some traitorous cueballs who thought that carpet-wielding was worth all the fuss.

Elton John

The short-fused singer fought a well-publicised battle against hair loss throughout the seventies and eighties, with a series of hats, hair transplants and even the odd three-foot-tall periwig. These days, however, he sports a more traditional rug, and candles are the last things he should be worrying about in the wind.

Judges

Keepers of a tradition surviving from the eighteenth century, judges are still required to wear large grey curly wigs in court. And while it's certainly tempting to try the usual rug quips on them, such as suggesting that they keep their hair on, telling them not to flip their wig or asking if they've been to Carpet World recently, this will almost certainly hinder your trial. Best to keep quiet.

Elizabeth I

The unsurprisingly virgin queen wore a wig after all her hair fell out when she washed it with the caustic cleaning solution lye. This inspired a trend for similar hairpieces among women of the time.

It's hard to imagine fashion being swayed by the royals in quite the same way these days. Which is just as well, as we'd all be wearing false ears to look like Charles, huge teeth to look like Camilla, and Nazi armbands to look like Prince Harry.

Mary Queen of Scots

Elizabeth's cousin Mary was also a renowned wiggie. It's thought that after her head was chopped off in 1587, her executioner tried to hold it up to show the crowd, only to find himself holding just her wig, while her head itself rolled along the floor. As far as rug mishaps go, this sounds even more embarrassing than having your syrup blow away in a gale. Although if you've just been beheaded, you probably wouldn't be that bothered about social shame.

King Louis XIV of France

The balding shortarse Sun King killed two birds with one stone by wearing incredibly tall hairpieces. If you're both vertically and follically challenged yourself, you might want to adopt his method, but remember that he, unlike you, could have anyone who took the piss out of his wig put to death.

Charles II of England

Upon his restoration to the throne in 1660, Charles II sparked a trend for curly black wigs among men eager to express their devotion to the king. It's a style that wouldn't be adopted again until over three centuries later, by men eager to express their devotion to guitar hero Brian May.

Are some ethnic groups more at risk from baldness than others?

It's true that racial variations in male pattern baldness have been found. Caucasians have the highest baldness rates, followed by Afro-Caribbeans, while Chinese and Japanese men have very low rates. It is incredibly rare for Native Americans to go bald naturally, although some tribes traditionally shaved off most of their hair anyway. It's quite heartening to know that man feels the need to invent baldness where it doesn't occur. It all goes to prove that the baldilocks image is naturally sexier.

Frankie Howerd

Although many wigs are said to look like dead animals, Frankie Howerd's was one of the few to be treated like one, when it was buried in his back garden after his death. Happily, however, it has now been exhumed and placed in a museum in Howerd's old house.

Paul Daniels

He could make audiences believe he was sawing Debbie McGee in half, but the so-called illusionist fooled no one into thinking that hair grew naturally on his head. After years of jibes from the tabloids and *Spitting Image*, Daniels decided to stop living the hair-lie in the late eighties, when he had a series of increasingly smaller and thinner wigs constructed before doing away with them altogether.

Humphrey Bogart

Off-screen, the movie legend was apparently more hard-boiled egg than hard-boiled detective. Luckily for Bogart, he had the best make-up artists in Hollywood attending to his hairpiece. Which is just as well, as it would probably have ruined the emotional ending of *Casablanca* had the plane propellers blown his hair off while he was saying his last goodbye to Ingrid Bergman.

Ruth Regina

Although not a wiggie, nor a name likely to be known to the uninitiated, Ruth Regina is notable for being the first ever wigmaker for dogs. On her website, www.ruthreginawigs.com, you can choose for your canine such styles as curly red hair, long straight brown hair or blonde pigtails. Although there is perhaps a case against bringing such a bizarrely needless product into the world, it should be pointed out in her defence that most of the dogs on her site look no more or less ridiculous than the average human rug-wearer.

the comb-over question

Many slapheads have considered covering their bare domes with a comb-over at some point. It's certainly easy to see why the option is so tempting to so many baldies. You won't have to spend money on rugs or drugs, you won't have to go through the pain of surgery, and if your hairstyle is unravelled by a strong wind, you can simply pretend you're going to a fancy dress party as Phil Oakey from The Human League.

If you're thinking of opting for a comb-over yourself, you might find the process more complicated than you expect. But by following this simple guide you'll achieve Bobby Charlton chic in no time.

First, decide which side of your head you want to comb from. Do you have a natural parting line on the left or the right? Is your hair slightly thicker on one side?

You should also consider alternatives such as combing from both sides and weaving the hair in the middle for a 'Shredded Wheat' effect, curling both sides around on top of your head to create the celebrated 'Walnut Whip' style, or even creating a 'comb-back' from a particularly bushy set of eyebrows like Denis Healey MP. But beware that these styles take a lot of skill and effort to manage, and should not be attempted by novices.

The next thing to decide is how far down the side of your head to start combing from. It's tempting to start right next to the bald patch itself, and try to pass off your comb-over as neatly parted hair. But if you do this, you'll only encounter the hassle of having to adjust your comb-over as you

the bald facts

Is fear of baldies a genuine condition?

'Peladophobia' is the term used to describe people with an intense and irrational fear of the bald. This is distinct from 'baldophobia', a term used to describe prejudice against the bald. Unlike those who are simply envious of gleaming pates, peladophobics suffer from a medical disorder that makes them experience intense panic whenever they see an unfurnished dome. But perhaps the shiny community should try to help these people rather than condemn them. One of the treatments for phobias is called 'flooding' and involves immersing the sufferer in their fear until it goes away. So if you know a peladophobic, why not organize a bald surprise party for them? Simply arrange for all the slapheads you know to hide in their house and then jump out at them at the same time as eating boiled eggs, playing Right Said Fred songs and waving pictures of Kojak. It's bound to work.

recede. It's probably better to go for the full 'Arthur Scargill' right now and start combing from just above the ear.

As you guide your hair across the vast, gleaming expanse of your noodle, take a moment to decide how to style it on top. Some men like to shampoo, condition and then blow-dry their hair so that it takes on the fluffy texture of a small woodland creature. But the true enthusiast will tell you that it's not a proper comb-over unless it's greasily matted down to your skull. Therefore, when you've finished combing, and the left and right sides of your hair are reunited at last, you need to make sure you've got the right fixing agent to secure your hair in place. A firm gel, mousse or

CAST-IRON COMB-OVER SPRAY

spray will probably do the trick, although more extreme comb-over merchants have been known to resort to egg white.

The obvious disadvantage of a comb-over, of course, is that it only works for as long as you have some kind of hair on your head to sweep across. But the true Captain Comb-over will always find a way. Even the tiniest fertile patch can be swept around the entire skull with considerable planning and skilful hair engineering.

BALD SPOT

'We're all born bald, baby.'

Telly Savalas, actor

the baldie hall of shame:
comb-over merchants

The much-maligned comb-over style has given us some truly breathtaking feats of hair construction over the decades. Here we salute the men who've cured their own baldness with nothing more than a comb, a mirror and a massive dose of self-deception.

Napoleon Bonaparte
Like *Call My Bluff* presenter Robert Robinson (see the next page), Bonaparte adopted the comb-forward style as his hairline retreated, giving him the permanent appearance of someone whose hair has been matted to his forehead by heavy rain. Unlike Robert Robinson, however, he vented his frustration about his ridiculous hair by invading various countries including Italy, Malta, Poland and Russia.

Neil Kinnock
Kinnock tried to unite the divided factions within both his hair and the Labour Party in the eighties. But in both cases the gulf was too wide for his attempts to look convincing.

Julius Caesar

Another invader who favoured the comb-forward style was Julius Caesar. However, Caesar wisely took to covering his ridiculous style in public with a series of elaborate laurel wreaths, using the ruse of distracting attention from baldness with silly headgear (a technique later employed by Elton John).

Robert Robinson

Archive evidence shows that the *Call My Bluff* presenter's hairstyle was technically a 'comb-forward', starting as it did at the back of the head, thus avoiding the awkward semi-circular bald patch that side-combing can leave. But however we wish to label Robinson's hair, it's an undeniably striking work of hair sculpture and almost avant-garde in its lack of convincingness.

Jack and Bobby Charlton

Do you have a job that involves running around and hitting a spherical object with your head, often in adverse weather conditions? Well, why not cultivate a hairstyle that can't withstand the slightest breeze? That won't become such an in-joke that it overshadows your entire career, will it?

Desmond Morris

The TV-presenter ethologist once claimed that baldness was a 'human display signal indicating male dominance' because it was linked with high levels of sex hormones. Which doesn't quite explain why he spent the seventies and eighties sporting a greasy thin comb-over, which is surely a human display signal indicating that you're an idiot.

The Baldie Man

Technically the character of 'Baldie Man' from the sketch show *Naked Video* should have been called 'Comb-over Man', as much of the humour in his segments centred around his doomed attempts to keep his greasy strands neatly arranged on the top of his head. His most famous appearance was in an ad for Hamlet cigars, where he struggled vainly to arrange his hair in a photo booth. Such bald-baiting seems especially rich coming from a tobacco company, as some studies have suggested a link between smoking and baldness. Surely the last thing Baldie Man should have been doing was putting his few remaining hairs at risk by lighting up.

Arthur Scargill

Former National Union of Mineworkers leader Scargill's huge orange comb-over might have looked like fresh roadkill, but it was in fact a clever piece of political manipulation. 'Look at me,' it said to the working man, 'I've created this thing on my head through years of honest toil. I haven't ponced around spending money on wigs or Minoxidil. I just pick up a comb, roll up my sleeves and get on with the hard graft.'

Donald Trump

If you want proof that the comb-over is truly the greatest baldness solution, look no further than Donald Trump. He could afford a truckload of every cure that's ever been invented, but instead he chooses to be seen with an unconvincing fluffy object hovering above his skull. Trump has uttered his catchphrase 'You're fired' countless times on *The Apprentice*, but surprisingly it seems he has never said it to his hairdresser.

Teachers

Before the fashion for cropped hair in the nineties, an extraordinary number of teachers unwisely plumped for the comb-over style. This led to the popularity of a game called 'Tilt the Comb-over', which involved trying to make your teacher so angry that the trembling of his head would cause his comb-over to flap open, thus exposing his pate to the class. The winner would be the pupil who finally sent the teacher over the edge into a hair-destabilizing rage. It was a game that carried the risk of serious punishment, but it was worth it for the slapstick entertainment value.

Rudy Giuliani

Former mayor of New York City who, after September 11, stood firm and unflappable in the face of international terrorism. As did the thin veneer of hair covering the top of his head, which looked like it was held in place with industrial glue. Although Giuliani has now been forced to abandon his comb-over by style advisors, few will forget the days it sat steadfastly on his head as a poignant symbol of the freedom, enjoyed in the West, to sport unconvincing hair.

keep it under your hat

Although wearing headgear at all times is both rude and a shameful denial of baldness, there are certain circumstances, such as during heat waves and torrential downpours, in which covering up your pate is a good idea. Here are some options for the modern pilgarlic.

Baseball caps

The most popular choice for slapheads these days seems to be the baseball cap. Although cheap and easily available, baseball caps can lead to accusations of trying to look cooler or younger than you are. These claims were levelled at William Hague in 1997, when he was snapped wearing a baseball cap in a theme park and accused of trying to chase the youth vote. But you have to feel some sympathy for Hague here – covering up your pate on the log flume is hardly on a level with buying an iPod and pretending to like Kanye West.

Ultimately, the acceptability of baseball caps comes down to context.

Wearing a plain cap on a hot day, for example, is fine. Wearing a fake Von Dutch cap at a 45-degree angle, pulling your trousers down so the top of your underwear is exposed, clicking your fingers and shouting 'dat is nang, blud', is not.

Bandanas
Popular with wrestlers, aging rockers and Eastern European peasants, bandanas can be a tempting option for the barnet-less. But be careful where you wear them. In some urban areas of the US certain colours of bandana are associated with particular gangs, so you could be at risk of a drive-by shooting. Cheap and effective they may be, but bandanas are not worth risking your life for.

Cowboy hats
Western fans might be tempted to cover their pates with a classic Stetson. But you should be aware that this item of headgear carries different connotations depending on your environment. Worn down to your local pub's line-dancing

night, a cowboy hat will signify nothing more than your love of country music. However, worn in certain areas of town, it could mark you out as a 'confirmed bachelor'. Especially if it's worn in conjunction with a tight T-shirt and a pair of crotchless leather chaps.

Berets

Sadly, the beret is a piece of headgear that seldom creates the effect its wearer desires. You might think that you look like a rock-hard Special Forces soldier. But to others, you will simply look French. And surely no one can be so ashamed of their baldness that they'd rather anyone thought *that* about them.

Hoodies

Rather than going to the effort of buying a hat, you could simply pull the hood from your sweatshirt over your head. But there are some serious disadvantages to this. For a start, you could be accused of trying to look hipper than you really are. Also, anyone walking in front of you at night might think you're planning to mug them. And perhaps most worryingly of all, there's a danger that David Cameron will try to hug you. So, all in all, it's probably better to look like a happy slaphead than a happy slapper.

Do-rags

If baseball caps aren't urban enough for you, you could always wear a do-rag such as those that gangsta rappers like 50 Cent sport. A do-rag is a small nylon mesh designed to fit snugly around the hair and keep it in place. Originally worn to protect afros, do-rags have recently achieved widespread popularity, and must be pretty tempting for the chrome boy who wants to be a homeboy. But unless you're prepared to go all the way with your ghetto styling and wear low-rise jeans, prison-white sneakers and more bling than Jimmy Savile, it's best to steer clear.

Bowler hats

If you're worried that a baseball cap or a hoodie might make you look like you're too try-hard, why not go to the other extreme and look like someone from the nineteenth century? It's been a while since bowler hats were in fashion, but there's no reason why you shouldn't try to revive them. You'll certainly be popular with American tourists who believe that everyone in England still swans around with such a headpiece perched daintily on their bonce.

Deerstalkers

Sick of being compared to the fictional detective Kojak? Then this is probably not the hat for you. If, however, you're a fan of Sherlock Holmes, a deerstalker can be a good option. It protects your face and neck, you can use the side flaps to cover your ears and you'll be the first person everyone turns to if there's a mysterious murder that baffles the police.

Top hats

Now this is more like it. If you're going to wear a hat you might as well be unapologetic and go for the most noticeable one. Although little seen these days, top hats were widely accepted in the nineteenth century. Abraham Lincoln used to wear a massive one known as a 'Stovepipe', and they let him be in charge of a country. Admittedly, top hats might be harder to carry off in modern times, but if Noddy Holder and Slash from Guns N' Roses can work them into their look, so can you.

BALD SPOT

'Bald as the bare mountain tops are bald, with a baldness full of grandeur.'

Matthew Arnold, poet and critic

the baldie hall of fame:
baldie blasts from the past

Not all baldies have achieved the lasting fame of Shakespeare or Aristotle. In this section we honour some of the forgotten slapheads who shone briefly – but no less brightly.

Bod
A staple of seventies and eighties kids' telly, Bod employed a minimalist animation style before the creators of *South Park* were even born. It was never quite explained why Bod himself was so perfectly bald. He seems old enough to have grown hair, too young to have lost it, and there was little in his gently hallucinogenic world to make you suspect balding due to stress, although I suppose that seeing Alberto Frog and his Amazing Animal Band could be a bit disconcerting.

Sloth from *The Goonies*
Although he initially appears to be scary, Sloth turns out to be a goodie in *The Goonies*, and the movie's kids learn not to be misled by his physical deformities. Which is all well and

good, but why did they have to make baldness one of these 'deformities'? Thanks to him, many baldies with droopy eyes and sticky-out ears still get called 'Sloth' today.

'Bullet' Baxter

PE teacher from *Grange Hill* whose bald crown and bushy beard made him look like his head was upside down. Perhaps it was his association with PE that led to the seventies' playground craze of forming a punctured football into a dome shape, placing it on your head as a makeshift bald cap and pretending to be 'Bullet' Baxter.

Interestingly, the word 'bullet' is now used in the US to mean 'receding long hair', but this is a portmanteau of 'balding' and 'mullet' rather than because the strict PE teacher had somehow gathered a cult following there.

Chad

'Chad' is the name given to the UK's second most popular graffiti drawing, after a cock and balls. It features a baldie sticking his long nose over a fence and is typically accompanied by a slogan such as 'wot no bread?' Chads were at the height of their popularity during post-war rationing, when there were plenty of things to complain about the lack of. Their appeal has waned since then, but they live on in the hands of children who are rebellious enough to draw graffiti, but not quite rebellious enough to draw something obscene.

Charlie Brown

Although *Peanuts* creator Charles M. Schultz claimed that Charlie Brown was supposed to have very light hair rather than none at all, many took his insistent cries of 'good grief', 'rats' and 'why can't I have a normal dog like everybody else?' as evidence of stress-related alopecia.

Dungeon Master

Tiny comb-dodging mentor from eighties' cartoon *Dungeons and Dragons* who gave cryptic advice to a group of American teenagers that were transported into a fantasy realm by a faulty rollercoaster. As well as giving the world yet another insulting term for baldies, Dungeon Master taught an entire generation to regard the utterances of shortarsed baldies as deep and profound, however meaningless they might at first seem. Which may explain why so many of them have subsequently risen to managerial positions.

Elmer Fudd

The *Looney Tunes* star didn't let his speech impediment and baldness hinder his career as a rabbit hunter. What did hinder his career as a rabbit hunter, however, was wasting all his time pursuing one particular wisecracking rabbit from New York instead of going after the more docile, non-speaking variety usually found in abundance in the wild.

Hufty
Domeheaded lesbian presenter of nineties 'yoof TV' car crash *The Word*. Not to be confused with road-safety squirrel Tufty, who was heterosexual. Although he did have a very close friendship with Willy the Weasel, come to think of it.

Pac Man
Eighties' arcade icon Pac Man was probably hairless due to technological restrictions rather than design, but he remains an icon for the bald fraternity nonetheless. Originally called 'Puck Man' in Japan, his name was changed when he was exported to the US to thwart Tippex-wielding vandals. Pac Man became a global phenomenon as well as a role model for the rave generation, who decided that listening to repetitive bleeps and eating lots of pills looked like fun.

The Mekon
The arch-enemy of Dan Dare who appeared in weekly comic *The Eagle*. The Mekon was the ruler of the Treens of Northern Venus and had a huge green head. The nickname 'Mekon' is still used to describe baldies with especially bulbous foreheads today, and was used to taunt both William Hague and Sven-Göran Eriksson by their detractors.

Michael Fish
The BBC weather forecaster was always happy to display his nude pate without recourse to hats or wigs. Which is just as well because, as he proved before the great storm of 1987, his ability to predict high winds left something to be desired.

The Mole Men
In the Marvel Comics series, Superman encountered a race of small, balding partially sighted creatures called the 'Mole Men' who lived underground. Now, I'm not saying that the old wives' tales about a particular activity stunting your growth, making you go blind and causing hair loss are true. But if they are, I dread to think what these dirty bastards were up to before Superman discovered them.

Yoda

Slapheaded green Jedi Master who appears in all the Star Wars films except for the first one (or *Episode IV: A New Hope* as nerds call it). Yoda's enduring popularity means that his name is still used as an insult for shortarsed baldies today. To which the correct response is, 'Punch you in the face if you don't stop calling me that, I will.'

baldie health warning

Sadly, being a proud comb-dodger carries some health risks that are even more serious than getting repeatedly tapped on the head by a gang of crazed Benny Hill fans. For example, baring your naked dome to the sun can increase your risk of getting skin cancer, as your bonce will be directly exposed to harmful ultraviolet rays. It's very important, therefore, that you keep your head covered on hot days. Obviously, this doesn't mean you should resort to the shameful practices of wearing wigs and combing over, but wearing a hat on a boiling summer day is perfectly acceptable. Unless the hat in question is a novelty baseball cap bearing a slogan such as 'Official tan-line inspector', 'Will swap wife for beer' or 'I'm not as think as you drunk I am'.

If you're such a militant baldie that you refuse to cover your head at any time, you should at least rub in a high-factor suncream. It's probably better to be on the safe side and go as high as SPF 50, especially if you've shaved your head recently. If you're out sunbathing, remember to re-apply your suncream at regular intervals throughout the day. A good rule of thumb is that if your head stays so shiny that anyone who sits next to you has to put their sunglasses on, you're probably safe. Also, try to avoid being outside for the hottest part of the day, when the locals head indoors to leave the pissed-up holidaymakers to fry in the sun. And for God's sake try not to fall asleep with your crown exposed. Bald haters already have enough ammunition as it is. Don't make things easier for them by looking like something worn on Comic Relief day.

While we're on the subject of pate protection, you should also try to avoid staying on a sunbed for too long, as the strong rays can damage your skin. Although it's beyond me why any baldie would want to go to a tanning salon in the first place. Do you really want to look like a cross between Morph from *Take Hart* and the orange bloke from the old Tango ads?

50

BALDIE
FACTOR
FIFTY

the baldie ball of fame:
thin on top of the pops

From the mop tops of the Fab Four to the gravity-defying sculptures of A Flock of Seagulls, hair is as much a part of pop as the music itself. Surely there can be no room for baldies here? In fact, there have been a few music stars who understood that less is more when it comes to choosing a distinctive hairstyle.

Phil Collins

The amount of hair on top of the Genesis star's head has always been directly proportional to the progressiveness of his music. So, if Collins had a lot of hair, expect songs about dragons, and long instrumental sections. If he had no hair expect earnest songs about divorce and the homeless. Collins was one of those men whose temples increase leaving a narrow strip of hair on the top of the head resembling a tidily trimmed quim. It's appropriate, then, that by the time Genesis recorded 'The Brazilian' in 1986, that's exactly what he appeared to sport on his head.

Isaac Hayes

The smooth-skulled soul star was proud enough of his dome to display it prominently on the cover of his classic album *Hot Buttered Soul*. Hayes is also a successful actor, most famously as the voice of Chef in *South Park*, which he quit in 2005 after an episode mocked his religion, Scientology. Curiously, though, he never seemed to have an issue with the show's offensively baldophobic depiction of the character Mr Garrison.

Brian Eno

Rock would be a much less interesting place if it hadn't been for ambient pioneer, super-producer and Roxy Music star Brian Eno. In fact, Eno is so cool that he even managed to get away with combining long thinning hair and make-up in the early seventies. This is probably not an image you should attempt yourself, however. Just because it was acceptable on *Top of the Pops* in 1972, it doesn't mean you'll be able to get away with it on an industrial estate in Swindon today.

Various techno slapheads

There's never been a more domehead-friendly genre than dance music, with Orbital, Fatboy Slim, Moby and Karl Hyde from Underworld all pushing forward the boundaries of electronic music as their hairlines push back. Although considering that a bald smiley was adopted as an early icon of rave music, it shouldn't really be a surprise that so many slapheads were drawn to the genre.

Sinead O'Connor

O'Connor outraged middle England and earned the nickname 'Skinhead O'Connor' when she shaved her head in the late eighties. She caused further outrage when she ripped up a picture of Pope John Paul II live on American TV in 1992. This incident caused deep divisions within the bald community, who couldn't decide whether their loyalties lay with wannabe-baldie O'Connor or the Pope, who was a natural slaphead but always kept his crown covered.

Britney Spears

When pop temptress Spears shaved her head in 2007, the incident generated more media coverage than most international wars. And of all the pundits yadda-ing on about how it was a cry for help and a rebellious rejection of her manufactured image, not one of them considered that she might simply have realized that the cue ball look is sexier.

Michael Stipe

The Samson of alternative rock, REM frontman Stipe released the classic albums *Out of Time* and *Automatic for the People* while hirsute, but could only manage the sub-par *Monster* by the time he was hairless. Ironically, Stipe recorded 'Shiny Happy People' when he still had hair, but refuses to perform it now. Perhaps the title is just a bit too close to home these days.

Bald Elvis

In 2006, depilated Elvis tribute act Geraint Benny received death threats from hardcore fans who believed he was disrespecting the memory of The King. So let's get this straight, Elvis fans. Wearing a white jumpsuit when you're ridiculously obese is all right, but being bald isn't?

Right Said Fred

Novelty act featuring brothers Richard and Fred Fairbrass, who typified the bald 'Muscle Mary' look also seen on Richard from *Big Brother 7*. The Fairbrass brothers made their shiny heads look especially good by standing next to guitarist Rob Manzoli, who had an astoundingly misguided bubble-perm mullet.

Four Bitchin' Babes

Although not tonsorially challenged themselves, this female folk quartet did give the world the most explicitly pro-slaphead song ever. 'Bald Headed Men', released in 1993, details how they prefer chrome domes to 'big-haired boys' because they're more honest and they 'accept who they are'. While it might be tempting to choose this track for a special occasion such as the first dance at your wedding, remember that there are several better tracks with a similar message, such as 'The Shining' by Badly Drawn Boy, 'Shine On' by The House of Love, and 'I'll Be Your Mirror' by The Velvet Underground.

Michael Eavis

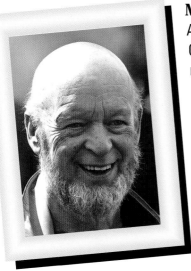

Although not technically a pop star, Glastonbury festival organizer Eavis has made a significant contribution to rock. He's also made a significant contribution to slaphead fashion with his beard-but-no-moustache image that makes him look like one of those pictures that still looks like a face when you turn it upside down.

jokes that are always made about baldies

It's been a long time since baldophobic travesties like *The Benny Hill Show* were accepted as popular entertainment, but still the weary ribbing continues. Don't be surprised if you hear some of these hair-loss quips next time you're out and about.

Your shiny head is blinding people
Perhaps the most popular joke amongst wags is to shield their eyes from your pate as if it's reflecting bright light. Far from being an original gag, this can even be traced back as far as Chaucer's *The Canterbury Tales*, in which a monk's bald head is described as 'shining like a mirror'. More recently, it featured in the 1987 novelty single 'Snooker Loopy' by Chas and Dave, in which they claim that the light reflecting from Willie Thorne's head dazzles other players into making mistakes. This joke is still sometimes recalled around pub pool tables by those unafraid to steal their material from Chas and Dave.

Your head can somehow be used as a mirror
Building on the shiny theme, some jokers will go on to claim that your head is actually a reflective surface, and one that they can even use to check their own reflection and (irony ahoy) arrange their hair.

Your head makes a squeaky noise

Some jokers will mime polishing your head and make a squeaking noise as if cleaning a window. It's never quite clear why a nude skull should be any squeakier than any other hairless part of the body.

Your face is getting longer

A more lateral way for would-be jokers to draw attention to your receding hairline. As in, 'Have you noticed how his face is getting bigger? It goes all the way up to here now,' or 'Why the long face?'

You shower bottle-free

In 1989, Proctor and Gamble launched a combined shampoo and conditioner onto the market with the slogan, 'Take two

bottles into the shower? Not me – I just Wash and Go!' This sent the country's amateur humorists into overdrive with yet another 'hilarious' baldie jibe: 'Take two bottles into the shower? Not [insert name of baldie here] – he doesn't take any!'

You have no use for hairdressers or styling products
As in sarcastic enquires such as, 'What conditioner do you use, mate?' or 'Can you recommend a good barber?'

You need to keep your hair on
Bald-baiters will knowingly use phrases with the word 'hair' in to annoy you. So you'll be told to 'let your hair down' at the office party, to stop 'tearing your hair out' when you're frustrated and to 'keep your hair on' when you get annoyed by all this ribbing. At which point you'll ask your tormentors to stop, and they'll reply, 'Sorry, I didn't realize I was getting in your hair' or 'What's the matter? Having a bad-hair day?'

You have the same hairstyle as a baby
This observation is especially common when others are inspecting your offspring. 'He's got the same hairstyle as his dad,' the wags will say, pointing to the infant's developing hairline.

One baldie who was especially plagued by this weak piece of whimsy was Winston Churchill, whose large face and heavy jowls made the

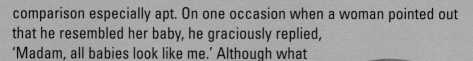

comparison especially apt. On one occasion when a woman pointed out that he resembled her baby, he graciously replied, 'Madam, all babies look like me.' Although what he really wanted to say was, 'Oh yeah, like I haven't heard *that one* before.'

You don't like to use the term 'bald'

'He's not bald', they will say in a jocular imitation of political correctness, 'he's follically challenged'. Or 'differently hirsute'. Or 'comb-averse'. Or 'involuntarily parted'. Or 'a person of restricted styling options'. Or perhaps they'll point at your temples and say, 'That's not a receding hairline, that's an advancing headline.'

Whatever teasing you're subjected to, the best thing you can do is state your pride about your baldness. That way your tormentors will realize that they haven't found a sensitive spot, and they'll probably just give up. If you ever get stuck, simply read aloud the handy cut-out-and-keep bald-pride speech below:

'I'm not follically challenged, I'm a baldie, a slaphead, a chrome dome, a cue ball, a boiled egg and a bald eagle. I'm a barber-dodging baldilocks who takes no bottles into the shower and *I am not ashamed!*'

BALD SPOT

'As a potent man comes to maturity, the testosterone begins to kill off the hair on top of his head. As he advances into vigorous middle age, his head rises through his remaining hair like a shining symbol of his virility.'

Clive James, writer and broadcaster

the baldie hall of fame:
bald sex symbols

Finally, after decades of being considered as attractive as halitosis, it seems that baldness is now sexy. Perhaps it's because men who parade their hairlessness exude self-confidence. Perhaps it's because women know they'll get more space in the bathroom cabinet if they marry a baldie. But whatever the reason, here are some of the slaphead sexpots who prove that bald is beautiful, glabrous is glamorous and skin is in.

Bruce Willis

Although rumoured to have been oversensitive about his thinning crown in the eighties, Willis became an evangelist for the bald cause after he shaved his head for *Pulp Fiction* in 1994. Since then he's become the quintessential baldie action star, and Terry Gilliam has described his head as 'a monument to cranial architecture'. If you called him a 'slaphead' he'd probably kick the shit out of you, smirk, and mutter a punning quip.

Roundness: 5
Shininess: 5
Smoothness: 3
Overall slaphead sex factor: 4

Andre Agassi

If you need proof of the transformational power of baldness, you only need to compare the woeful flaxen mane that Andre Agassi sported when he won Wimbledon in 1992 to the smooth pate he presents to the world these days. Back then he looked like a soft-metal fan who should be using his racket with which to mime an Eddie Van Halen solo. Now he's a shining example of chrome-domed sophistication.

Roundness: 3
Shininess: 4
Smoothness: 3
Overall slaphead sex factor: 3

Vin Diesel

The natural successor to Bruce Willis's uncovered crown, Diesel has played a huge part in making baldness sexy in recent years.

A baldie so tough his name is actually an anagram of 'I end lives', Diesel claims he deliberately shaves his head to cultivate the bald look, but it's more likely that hair is simply too afraid to grow on his head.

Roundness: 4
Shininess: 4
Smoothness: 4
Overall slaphead sex factor: 4

Michael Jordan

If you said the name 'Jordan' to an American, the chances are they wouldn't think of a troubled Middle-Eastern country or a sour-faced glamour model with plastic tits, but a bald basketball legend. The aerodynamically-skulled athlete was named as the greatest sportsman of the twentieth century by ESPN and one of the ten most beautiful people in the world by *People* magazine. He even picked up extra bald cred by appearing in the 1996 film *Space Jam* alongside fellow slapheads Elmer Fudd and Porky Pig. Jordan's contribution to making hairlessness sexy is so significant that he can even be forgiven for making ridiculously long basketball vests fashionable as an item of street wear.

Roundness: 5
Shininess: 5
Smoothness: 5
Overall slaphead sex factor: 5

Sean Connery

Although the James Bond series has been accused of baldophobia in its portrayal of the character Ernst Blofeld, Connery himself is a perennial hairless heartthrob. A proud pilgarlic, Connery makes about as much effort to hide his baldness as he does to change his

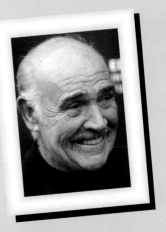

accent for the particular role he's playing.
Roundness: 3
Shininess: 4
Smoothness: 3
Overall slaphead sex factor: 3

Billy Corgan from Smashing Pumpkins

While goth pin-ups traditionally had gravity-defying barnets that made them look like they'd just woken up from an especially enjoyable bad dream, Smashing Pumpkins singer Billy Corgan shows that you can be both sexy and scary with no hair at all. With his smooth head, pale skin and black clothing, Corgan is the pop equivalent of Jack Skellington from *The Nightmare Before Christmas* and proves that you don't need big hair to join the miserable gang.
Roundness: 4
Shininess: 5
Smoothness: 4
Overall slaphead sex factor: 4

BALD SPOT

'Eggheads of the world unite. You have nothing to lose but your yolks.'
Adlai Stevenson, politician

Samuel L. Jackson

With his wondrously shiny pate, badass baldhead Jackson is proof of how much cooler men in their fifties can look when they shave their hair off entirely. His hairless roles include Jedi Master Mace Windu in the *Star Wars* prequels, who surely ranks alongside Yoda and genuine chrome-dome C3PO as one of the saga's best baldies.

Roundness: 5
Shininess: 4
Smoothness: 5
Overall slaphead sex factor: 5

Yul Brynner

When Brynner shaved off his few remaining strands to play the Siamese King in *The King and I*, a genuine baldie icon was born. With his perfectly smooth and spherical head, Brynner remains for many the definitive slaphead sex symbol, and is even referenced in a rhyme devised to comfort the receding:

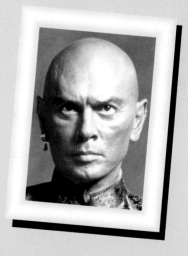

'If the hair on your head is
getting thinner
Don't despair, just think Yul Brynner.'

Roundness: 5
Shininess: 5
Smoothness: 5
Overall slaphead sex factor: 5

Demi Moore and various baldie women

It's not just blokes who can increase their sex appeal by shaving their heads. You only need to look at Demi Moore in *GI Jane*, Sigourney Weaver in *Alien³*, Natalie Portman in *V for Vendetta*, Samantha Morton in *Minority Report* and Sinead O'Connor in the video for 'Nothing Compares 2 U' for evidence of sexy slapheaded women. Perhaps as the human race heads towards its chrome-domed future, baldness will become accepted as the model of female attractiveness, and the head will become yet another area that men would like women to shave.

Roundness: 4
Shininess: 3
Smoothness: 3
Overall slaphead sex factor: 3

the curse of secret santa

Sadly, baldies are all too easy to shop for in the office Secret Santa. Typically, your name will be drawn by some bloke you've only spoken to a couple of times. With no private jokes to refer to, he turns his satirical energies to your most prominent feature – your shiny pate.

Unless he has the good sense to buy this book, he pops down to the shops and faces by an entire range of 'hilarious' bald-themed gifts to give to you at the Christmas party. His first option is buy an object that resembles an unfurnished head in some way. This might be a billiard ball, but this could easily turn into a makeshift weapon by being placed in a sock if you were to take the joke the wrong way. So he'll probably opt for something safe like a ping-pong ball, a grapefruit, a light bulb, a Kojak-style lollipop or the classic boiled egg.

A popular option for the less adventurous colleague would be an item of Homer Simpson merchandise, such as a tie, fridge magnet or beer glass. While these items probably won't cause much offence, most baldies have seen them all before, and the office joker is unlikely to get the laughter he craves.

His next option would be to buy some kind of cleaning product for your shiny pate such as Mr Sheen, Brasso or the intrinsically hilarious Cillit Bang. He might even add some kind of cleaning cloth, just in case the reference proves too subtle. If you're presented with a gift such as this at your Christmas party, be sure to bin it at an early stage of the evening, in case you pass out later on and the temptation to actually polish your head proves too much for your pissed-up colleagues to resist.

Perhaps the office joker will go for the re-growth angle. Regaine and Finisteride will prove too expensive, but he'll be able to get his hands on a dodgy herbal remedy, a bottle of Baby Bio or a packet of Miracle-Gro without going over the Secret Santa budget.

Then there's the ironic approach of shampoo, conditioner, spray, gel, wax, mousse, styling foam, combs, brushes, dye, hairdryers, curling tongs or home perming kits. As with cleaning products, these are dangerous things to have at a Christmas party, as whoever passes out first will almost certainly have them applied to their heads. However, as you're not at risk of being the victim in this case, you don't have to worry about leaving them lying around.

The last option, and sadly the most popular, is to buy a wig. Novelty wigs such as afros, mullets and bubble perms are available from joke shops

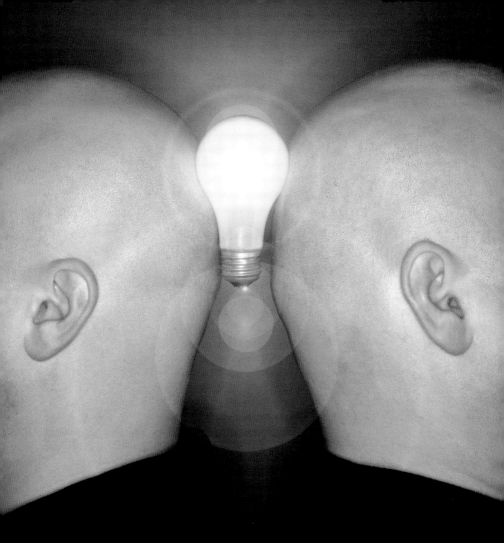

everywhere, and office pranksters will be drawn to them like flies to shit. If you do receive one this Christmas, complain that you're being discriminated against on the grounds of your physical appearance and demand to be told the name of the person who bought it for you. And then make sure you draw their name next year so you can get them something even more offensive.

BALD

SPOT

'Men with great hair are the blondes of the male population: they may get more than their fair share of attention, but no one expects them to have read Hegel's *Philosophy of Right*.'

Toby Young, journalist and writer

baldness and positive discrimination

The issue of whether slapheaded bosses ought to discriminate in favour of fellow pilgarlics is a tough one. The 'bald-guy rule' of recruitment states that if you have to choose between a hirsute candidate and a hairless one with roughly equivalent CVs, you should choose the follically challenged one. The reason for this is because society supposedly gives many preferences to attractive people, so if a baldie has the same record as a non-baldie, their achievement is actually more impressive.

But there are a few obvious problems with this theory. Firstly, it assumes that the bald are less attractive than the hirsute, which, as we saw in the 'Bald Sex Symbols' section, is untrue. Also, the notion that baldness holds you back doesn't seem quite right these days. In fact, in certain jobs, baldness can infer a level of authority and expertise that can help you get taken seriously. It all depends what you want to do, really. If you want to be a doctor or a lawyer, it could help. If you want to star in the next L'Oreal ad, it probably won't.

At the end of the day, it's difficult to justify positive discrimination towards the bald. There's not enough evidence that they get treated badly enough to justify a deliberate hairless hiring policy. But, if you're a bare-crowned boss, and you find yourself drawn towards other baldie candidates (perhaps because you see yourself reflected in them), you might as well add another comb-dodger to the team.

If anyone questions your bald favouritism, it shouldn't be too hard to think of an excuse. For example, you could suggest that their naturally cooler heads require less air conditioning in the summer. Or, most convincingly of all, you could claim that they don't have to waste time arranging their hair before meetings and therefore achieve far greater levels of productivity.

BALD SPOT

'You collect your straggling hairs on either side, Marinus, endeavouring to conceal the vast expanse of your shining bald pate by the locks which still grow on your temples.'

Marcus Valerius Martialis,
Roman poet

the baldie hall of shame:
baldie baddies

Sadly, society's rampant baldophobia has meant that shiny pates are often used as a visual shorthand for villainy and evil. Here are some infamous chrome domes who have reinforced negative stereotypes.

Nosferatu

When, in the 1920s, German director F. W. Murnau couldn't get the rights to Bram Stoker's novel *Dracula*, he decided to film it anyway with a number of changes. One of these was to make the vampire a rodent-like baldie rather than a charming aristocrat.

The success of the film inspired a whole tradition of garlic-fearing pilgarlics such as Kurt Barlow from *Salem's Lot*, Lotte Lipp from *The League of Gentlemen* and undead Tory leader Michael Howard.

Ming the Merciless

Yet another bald comic villain, this time from *Flash Gordon*. The evil ruler of the unfortunately-named planet Mongo,

Ming had arched eyebrows, a goatee beard and an unfurnished pointy head. The term 'Ming the Merciless' is still used as a nickname for unhygienic baldies today.

Freddy Krueger from *A Nightmare on Elm Street*

Unusually, Krueger's baldness was caused by being burned to death by a mob of angry parents and then being brought back to life by demons to kill teenagers in their dreams rather than male pattern baldness. Krueger seems to be ashamed enough of his unfurnished pate to cover it up much of the time with a fedora hat. Which is odd, because he seems quite proud of his hideously scarred face, cutlery fingers and the dreadful puns he utters after killing teenagers.

Lex Luthor

DC Comics were guilty of blatant baldism with the character of Superman's nemesis Lex Luthor. Apparently, Luthor was left hairless by an accidental chemical spill when he was a teenager in Smallville. Luthor blamed Superman for the accident and dedicated his life to villainy. While it's certainly true that premature hair-loss can make men do strange things such as wearing wigs and rubbing herbal remedies into their crowns, there's very little evidence that it can drive them to do things like firing ballistic missiles into the San Andreas fault to cause an earthquake that will destroy California.

Egghead

Another comic book villain whose depiction smacks of baldophobia is Egghead from *Batman*, played by Vincent Price in the sixties TV series. Egghead perpetrated crimes using weapons such as laughing-gas eggs and would constantly trot out puns like 'egg-sactly', 'egg-celent' and 'egg-speriment'. All of which became egg-scruciating after about five seconds.

Unsurprisingly, there's been little pressure from fans to revive the character for the new Batman movies. Although if they did, I'm sure Patrick Stewart, Ben Kingsley and Britney Spears would be interested in playing him.

Dr Evil and Mini Me

Slaphead supervillain Dr Evil and his midget assistant Mini Me inspired much bald-baiting in the nineties. If you're a shorter-than-average baldie, and you're friends with a much taller baldie, you've probably been called 'Mini Me' at some point.

Benito Mussolini

Like Lex Luthor and Dr Evil, Mussolini was a baldie supervillain who planned world domination, perhaps to compensate for his follicle failure. Unfortunately, unlike Lex Luthor and Dr Evil, he was real, and ruined the baldie look for a generation who associated it with fascism.

The Mitchell Brothers

The notion that being bald makes you hard was popularized in the nineties by pub landlords Grant and Phil Mitchell from *EastEnders*. Like a less camp version of Right Said Fred, they hogged the pre-credit drumbeats with their shouty acting. Nobody in their right mind would risk getting into a fight or a staring contest with either of these two.

Aliens

Science-fiction authors have often used baldness to portray extraterrestrial life forms who are more evolved than humans. Unfortunately, this has lead to the many negative depictions of alien baldies who are hellbent on conquering humanity and administering anal probes. Receding director Steven Spielberg did something to redress the balance with films like *ET* and *Close Encounters of the Third Kind*, both of which portray barnet-less aliens who are more interested in being your friend than killing you or sticking things up your bum.

Mark Oaten MP

Married MP Oaten deserves his place in the hall of shame for blaming a lurid 2006 affair with a rent boy on his hair loss. He claimed that noticing his receding hairline in the mirror spurred a crisis that inspired his sexual shenanigans. In retrospect, perhaps he should have taken the more obvious mid-life crisis route of buying himself a convertible car or going on a gap year to Thailand.

Zinedine Zidane

He might be one of the greatest footballers ever, but Zidane's shiny head caused an international storm when it butted Marco Materazzi's chest in the final of the 2006 World Cup. There was speculation at the time that Materazzi might have goaded Zidane by insulting his family or his ethnicity, but nobody seemed to consider the far more likely possibility that the more hirsute Italian had simply teased the Frenchman about his bonce.

Mr Before

The star of baldness-cure ads since the nineteenth century, Mr Before portrays slapheads as miserable about their condition and is usually seen next to someone called Mr After, who is identical in every way except that he has hair and is much happier.

Aleister Crowley

Like Paul Daniels, Crowley was a magician who was proud to display his bald crown to the world. Unlike Paul Daniels, however, he practised black magic, which involved ritual sex and indulging in hard drugs. If only he was the one given a primetime BBC1 show.

Death

A personification of the inevitable end of all life, Death is so ashamed of his baldness that he keeps his hoodie pulled up over his head at all times. Which presumably means that he's also denied access to the Bluewater Shopping Centre in Kent.

Darth Vader from Star Wars

When his mask was removed at the end of *Return of the Jedi*, it was revealed that the Dark Lord of the Sith was in fact a baldie who looked like Uncle Fester from *The Addams Family*. This led many fans to suppose that premature hair loss caused Anakin Skywalker turned to the dark side of the force. However, when the prequels were released a few years later, it was revealed that the real reasons for Anakin's fall were the evil influence of Palpatine and the emotional scars left from befriending an annoyingly camp Rastafarian frog called Jar Jar Binks, and that his hair loss was in fact the result of falling into some molten metal.

Pinhead from *Hellraiser*

The villain of Clive Barker's horror franchise is completely bald except for a series of nails that have been driven into his head along a grid carved into his scalp. While ramming nails into your skull might seem a rather extreme method of distracting from hair loss, it's probably not much more odd-looking or painful than the average hair transplant, so let's not be too quick to judge the slapheaded Cenobite.

BALD SPOT

'The tenderest spot in a man's make-up is sometimes the bald spot on top of his head.'

Helen Rowland, journalist

baldness and culture

It's not a bad time to be a chromeboy right now. Hairless icons like Vin Diesel and Bruce Willis have made shininess sexy, and many hirsute men are shaving their heads out of choice to jump on the baldilocks bandwagon. But depilation has not always been so fashionable, and perceptions of it have varied drastically as cultural attitudes to hair have changed.

In some societies, such as that of ancient Egypt, baldies went largely unnoticed thanks to the fashion for head-shaving and wig-wearing. Roman men often cut their hair short too, although we know from accounts of both Caesar's and Caligula's shame about their retreating hairlines that baldophobia was rife even then.

Unfortunately, the link between short hair and Rome led to even greater baldism elsewhere, with both the Franks and the Goths associating long hair with bravery and strength. Presumably, therefore, head-shaving wouldn't have been an option in these cultures, however badly you were receding, which must have led to entire armies being populated by warriors who resembled Wolf from *Gladiators*. No wonder everyone was so scared of them.

Hair has been so important to some cultures that men have chosen death over baldness. In the seventeenth century Manchu invaders tried to force the Chinese, who traditionally did not cut their hair, to shave the tops

of their heads and tie the rest of their hair back. Thousands of Chinese died resisting the edict. It's difficult to imagine these days anyone fighting to the death to keep a hairstyle, although Emo kids do get a bit sulky if their parents tell them to get rid of the hair covering their eyes.

More recently, long hair became an expression of counter-cultural identity by the hippy movement in the sixties, which associated short hair with the military and the police. This made things especially difficult for those hippies whose hair opted to drop out shortly after they did. They then had the difficult choice of either cutting it short and looking like a tool of oppression, or sticking with long, receding hair and simply looking like a tool.

Since then, baldies have survived the spiky hair of the punk era, the multi-layered experiments of the New Romantics, and the blow-dried bouffants of the eighties to arrive in a gleaming era where hairless domes are in vogue. So next time you're admiring the perfect roundness of your head, or applying a fresh layer of moisturizer to your skull for extra shine, be thankful that you're not in the era of the Franks, the Goths or the Hippies.

the worst receding hairstyles

Sometimes self-deception and vanity can stop men from admitting that their hairline is heading north. This can lead to some truly disturbing hair-don'ts from those seeking to defer their membership to Club Bald. Should you see someone sporting one of these styles, encourage them to shave their remaining hair and come out of the slaphead closet once and for all.

The 'Punk's Not Dead' – aka the Last of the Mohican

A receding hairline can look especially sad on a former punk, given that the movement was supposed to be about youthful anarchy and 'no future'. Well, there was a future, and it brought a mortgage, kids and male pattern balding. John Lydon sported a tragic example of this style when he appeared on *I'm a Celebrity, Get Me Out of Here*, by which time he'd given up trying to smash the system in favour of swearing at ostriches.

Receding dreadlocks –
aka Exodus

Hair loss must be especially difficult for Rastafarians. Not only does long hair hold a religious significance for believers, but baldophobia is rampant in their faith, where the word 'baldhead' is used to refer to someone caught up in evil Western culture.

The receding mullet –
aka the Skullet (as well as the Bullet, the North Carolina Neck Warmer, the Kentucky Waterfall, the Mississippi Mudflap, and many other designations)

Sorry to break this to you, but growing your hair long at the back won't compensate for what's happening on top. In fact, it makes things much, much worse.

The receding 'big hair' –
aka the Fading Glory

As seen on glam-metal fans who still use hairspray, gel and backcombing to create huge flammable styles, despite a lack of cooperation from their temples. The hair equivalent of refusing to leave a party after everyone else has gone home. Seriously dudes – it's over.

The receding pony tail – aka the Steven Seagal

This unfortunate style represents yet another woeful attempt to compensate for what's happening on top by growing long what's left. As seen in the previous chapter, thousands of Chinese men chose death before this hairstyle when the Manchu occupiers tried to force them to adopt it in the seventeenth century. And looking at the yuppie throwbacks who favour it, you can kind of see their point.

The receding afro – aka the Halo

You have to feel for those who were losing their hair in the seventies. Every year hair was getting bigger, while their capacity to produce it was getting less. This lead to some very odd hairstyles including the balding afro, where men would try to draw attention away from their depleting hairlines by growing their remaining hair so big it trespassed on flight paths.

The receding quiff –
aka Elvis Has Left the Building

Although the quiff is a style that exposes receding hairlines especially mercilessly, fans of both Morrissey and Elvis seem especially reluctant to give it up. There surely comes a point, however, when receding quiff crosses the line into Mohican, and you start to look more like a midlife-crisis punk than a 1950s rebel.

The receding perm –
aka the Wave Goodbye

Ironically, the word 'perm' is actually an abbreviation of 'permanent', but those who adopt this style prove that it's anything but. In fact, perms themselves can sometimes cause hair loss (because the chemicals used in the process can inflame follicles), so this seems like an especially self-defeating hairstyle. Would you really rather look like an aging Scouser than display your lovely pate to the world?

The horseshoe – aka the Short Back and Sides and Even Shorter Top

Traditionally, keeping a fringe of short hair on the side and back of the head was the look that all baldies went for. But in this day and age of bald chic, it seems a little apologetic. Surely it's better to shave it all off and become a shining example of bald pride than hang on to the world of the hirsute in such a half-arsed fashion?

the baldie hall of shame:
receding celebrities

If you're thinking of trying something different with your few remaining strands, heed the following warnings. Hopefully they'll prove to you that it's better to be bald than balding.

Bert from *Sesame Street*

The yellow puppet suffered from a bizarre case of male pattern balding that left just a small tuft of hair on the very top of his very pointy head. Still, with his huge monobrow, wide mouth and closeted relationship with Ernie, he had more important things to worry about.

Peter Stringfellow

If you're a receding man who wants to date a series of beautiful girls less than half your age, you could follow Stringfellow's example and grow your hair long, bleach it and then blow-dry it so that it looks like the mane of an especially sleazy lion. It's probably best to check that you're a multi-millionaire who owns a chain of nightclubs before trying this, though.

Billy Crystal

With his curly hair halo, Crystal should take a tip from one of the awards he often gives out on Oscar night and present a gleaming dome to the world. Though he won over a legion of fans with *When Harry Met Sally*, only a mad person would say 'I'll have what he's having' if they saw him in the barbers now.

Bill Bailey

With his peculiar combination of beard, nude skull and rear hair-flap, Bailey looks more like a confused engineering lecturer than a TV star. With his aging hippy image now something of a trademark, he'll probably have to go through the rest of his career looking like the result of an unnatural union between a Hobbit and a Klingon.

Michael Bolton

The MOR crooner's textbook skullet made him look like a bald man emerging from a waterfall of curly hair. Thinning at the front but wild and loose at the back, Bolton's hair was a visual representation of the compromise between raunchiness and restraint that could be found in his music.

Art Garfunkel

While singing with Paul Simon in the sixties, Garfunkel nurtured the bizarre ginger afro hairstyle that wouldn't be seen again until *Napoleon Dynamite*. Even more bizarrely, he persevered with the look as his hair fell out in the seventies. By the time he was back in the charts with *Bright Eyes*, he looked like a bald man standing in front of an orange cloud.

Hulk Hogan

Although the wrestling star usually covers it up with a bandana or a baseball cap, Hogan has a fringe of mid-length blonde hair around his bald pate that he complements with a handlebar moustache. Still, if you could perform the full-body slam, the side headlock and the atomic leg-drop, you too could get away with looking this ridiculous.

William Shakespeare

Although he gave the English language countless words and phrases, and many enduring plays and poems, Shakespeare's influence on hairstyling has been much more limited. In fact, it wasn't until Max Wall and Hulk Hogan came along that any other celebrities would attempt his 'receding bob' haircut.

Benjamin Franklin

One of the Founding Fathers of the USA, Franklin didn't let his baldness stop him from growing his hair long and wavy at the back and sides. Although the right to bear this hairstyle isn't explicitly mentioned in the Constitution, Franklin's endorsement is permission enough for many Americans, and the style can still be seen on many middle-aged stoners who live with their parents and wear tie-dye T-shirts.

Father Time

An old man with a huge white beard and fluffy white hair at the back and sides, as seen in the painting *A Dance to the Music of Time* by Nicolas Poussin, as well as on *The Smurfs*. Admittedly, Father Time is a personification of an abstract notion rather than a real person, but that's no excuse for crap hair.

Terry Nutkins

Although the original presenter of *The Really Wild Show* has been off our screens for a few years now, his receding hairdo is fondly remembered by an entire generation. With its striking juxtaposition of long wavy strands at the back and exposed head, Nutkins's hair was every bit as rare and fascinating as the wildlife featured in the show.

Ron Jeremy

The infamous porn star has stuck with the same long, thinning, curly hair since his rise to fame in the seventies and it doesn't seem to have harmed his success with the female sex. Although it probably wasn't his hairstyle that these 'ladies' were admiring.

Graham Norton

If you're receding severely from the temples, it's probably best not to sculpt the hair left in the middle into a miniature quiff. And if you are going to do this, it's probably best not to dye this miniature quiff blonde while leaving the rest of your hair brown. And if you are going to do both of these things, it's probably best not to include a feature on your show that invites viewers to send in pictures of any 'hairstyle faux pas' they've spotted. It's a bit like getting 'Mad' Frankie Fraser to present *Crimewatch*.

David Crosby

The Crosby, Stills and Nash star's distinctive combination of long, floppy moustache and long, thinning hair makes him one of the easiest rock stars to draw, along with ZZ Top and Slash from Guns N' Roses. His celebrated 'aging hippy' hairstyle can still be seen on many members of his generation today. Although it's not always clear if these styles are intended as a conscious tribute to Crosby, or they're just kind of what happens to middle-aged men who are too stoned to go to the barbers.

BALD SPOT

'We like very much man who is bald. We say man who is bald have a big hram.'

Borat, Da Ali G Show

a guide to shaving your head

If learning about bald heritage has made you want to sever your last remaining ties with the hirsute and join the slaphead fraternity for real, then it's time to shave your head.

A lot of baldies are reluctant to shave their barnets totally nude, as they're worried that their heads are unusual shapes or that their ears will stick out too much. But while the totally hairless look might take a bit of getting used to, many slapheads are pleasantly surprised by the reaction they get. For example, by presenting your unfurnished dome to the world without apology you'll project self-confidence, which is always an attractive quality.

The first thing you need to do when removing your few remaining hairs is to chop them as short as possible. Given that the hairs don't have to be an even length, you can do this yourself with a pair of clippers. It can be quite satisfying to shed your hairs on purpose like this, as if to say 'I don't want you anyway, you fickle bastards.'

The next thing to do is wet your head and cover the area you're going to shave with cream or gel. You might find that it's better to start by removing the softer hairs on the top and sides of your head, to give the cream more time to soak into the thicker hair at the back. As for shaving direction, you'll get a closer result if you go against the grain of your hair, but you'll have less chance of irritation if you shave with it. Basically, as long as you don't shave sideways you'll be all right.

Try to shave slowly and accurately so that you won't have to go over the same area twice, as this can cause irritation. When you're done, wash your head with soap and then rinse it. It's a good idea to apply some kind of moisturizer when you're finished. Although the shine this creates might encourage pub wags to imply that looking at your head is like staring into the very heart of the sun, it will at least stop your skin from drying out. However, it's best to avoid adding an extra layer of shine with Mr Sheen or Brasso. Contrary to what baldie-baiters might tell you, these products are rarely used on the head.

Don't worry if the newly revealed areas of your scalp are slightly paler than the rest of your head. After a couple of days of exposure to sunlight, the tone of your scalp should match the rest of your head. Just remember to use suncream if it's hot, and try to resist the temptation to cover your head in fake-tan lotion. Yes, it will make your entire bonce a consistent colour. But the colour in question will be bright orange and you'll look like a space hopper.

Many baldies who shave their skulls in winter complain that they feel the cold a lot more than before. While it's true that hair provides insulation

the bald facts

How do I avoid getting a rash when shaving my head?

If your skin is especially sensitive to the touch of a razor you should shave your head slowly, in short strokes and in a downward motion, so that you're going with the grain of the hair rather than against it. Make sure you're using a sharp razor, and rinse it often in warm water. After you've finished shaving, you may find that a medicated aftershave or moisturizer can prevent rashes.

Some men find that they can avoid rashes if they use an electric shaver rather than a razor, whereas others simply find their skin is too sensitive, and give up on shaving their heads totally nude. If you're one of these unfortunates, please at least try to keep your hair cropped very short, rather than letting it devolve into an unkempt 'skullet' (see page 126).

against breezes, and you'll notice a change at first, you'll soon get used to it. You could always wear a hat if it's especially nippy.

Now all you have to do is repeat the shaving process every three or four days and you'll be a fully-fledged chrome dome, with a head so magnificently shiny that anyone who tries to photograph it will get an 'OVEREXPOSED' sticker on their picture when it comes back from the developers.

the future's bright

In our journey through bald culture, we've learned all about the contribution chrome domes have made to the world, and we've found plenty of reasons to take pride in the gleaming pate. But what does the future hold for baldies as we gaze into our crystal balls (or failing that, each other's heads)?

On one hand, given the amount of money that's currently getting ploughed into researching a cure for baldness, you may think that there's no future at all for the shiny-domed. Advances in genetic engineering mean that it could soon be possible to make follicles immune to the effects of the baldness-inducing hormone DHT. Some scientists even predict that this could lead to the first shampoo that actually prevents the user from going bald, which will presumably be called 'Slaphead 'n' Shoulders'.

But let's remember the bigger picture here. As we saw at the beginning of this book, man has gradually been losing hair as it has become less important to his survival. So it's not too much to imagine that eventually all humans will be hairless, and they'll look back at the hirsute as little more than knuckle-dragging cavemen. Which would mean that those brave pioneers who bare their pristine crowns to the world are actually ahead of their time.

And if all the world's receding men followed their shining example, the baldness-cure industry would collapse overnight and all those pharmaceutical companies wasting millions on finding a way to re-plant follicles could spend their time curing more important things. Like isolating and eradicating the gene that makes people think the nickname 'baldilocks' is amusing.

If this guide to bald heritage has helped you to feel better about your hairlessness, please encourage others to join the league of proud pilgarlics with you. Tell them that it's time for slapheads to ditch the drugs and plugs and unite in a brotherhood of baldness.

Together we can expose our gleaming domes to the world and lead mankind into a brighter, balder future.

the baldies' survival guide
spoon amnesty

Every day, thousands of innocent slapheads
across the world are subjected to spoon
attacks. These senseless acts typically involve
shouting at bald men the words 'boiled egg' and then tapping their heads
with spoons. Here at *The Baldies' Survival Guide* we strongly believe that
these acts of baldophobic violence should not be tolerated.
That's why we're asking you to hand in all your spoons to your
local police station in complete confidence. Please surrender
your spoons and let's get these weapons of hairless hatred off
our streets for good. Plus, if you know of anyone with baldist
tendencies whom you suspect of harbouring spoons,
encourage them to give them up.

Spread the word about the spoon amnesty and help us to
create a world where anyone, whatever their follicular status,
can walk around without fear of cutlery attack.

picture credits

Jupiter Images Corporation: p. 66

Topfoto.co.uk: pp. 47, 89, 120

www.shutterstock.com: pp. 8, 12,
14–16, 18–20, 31, 32, 35–6, 38, 40, 43,
52, 54, 56, 58, 10, 63, 68–9, 71–2, 78–9,
81–2, 91, 94, 99, 101, 110–11, 118, 123,
137, 139, 140–43

Rex Features: pp. 29, 45, 48–9, 50, 64,
73–6, 84, 87, 92–3, 95, 97, 103–105,
107, 115, 117, 130–2, 134

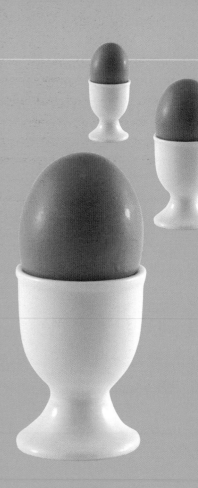